50

Awareness Activities
&
Tarot Games

Also by Heather Oelschlager

The BLUE DOOR MEDITATION SERIES:

Through the Blue Door:
A Medium's Guide to Ultra-Sensory Meditation & Journaling

Through the Blue Door Companion Journal
(E-book available exclusively at www.MandorlaAcademy.com/shop)

50

Awareness Activities
&
Tarot Games

Heather Oelschlager
Kefi Press

Copyright © 2020, Heather Oelschlager.

All rights reserved. No part of this book may be used or reproduced in any manner whatsoever for public or private use without prior written consent from the author and publisher, except in the case of reviewers using brief, attributed quotations embodied in a review.

The intent of the author is only to offer information of a general nature to help you in your quest for emotional and spiritual well-being. This book is not intended as a substitute for medical advice of physicians. The reader should consult a physician in matters relating to his/her/their health and particularly with respect to any symptoms that may require diagnosis or medical attention. In the event you use any of the information in this book for yourself, which is your constitutional right, the author and the publisher assume no responsibility for your actions.

ISBN 978-0-9997082-1-7 (Paperback Edition)

Library of Congress Control Number: 2020941369

Published by Kefi Press
PO Box 174
Hastings, MN 55033

Visit www.MandorlaAcademy.com

Cover design by Kai Oelschlager.
Book design and illustrations by Heather L. Oelschlager.
Original cover illustration by Heather L. Oelschlager.

9 8 7 6 5 4 3 2 1
First paperback edition July 2020
Printed in the United States of America

TABLE of CONTENTS

Introduction 15
    Get it Together List   16
    Tarot Deck Suggestions   20
    Pre-Tarot Games   22
        Major Arcana Worksheet   23
        Minor Arcana Worksheet   25

PART ONE | AWARENESS ACTIVITIES 29
    Activity Warm-Up   30
1 | Skip It: An Activity for Calm   31
2 | Biblio Takeaway   32
3 | Free and Clear   33
4 | Word-Fill to Find Insight   37
5 | I Get It   39
    I Get It; You Can, Too *   40
6 | Biblio Mania *   42
7 | Wish in the Wind: Activity for Hope   44
8 | Photojournalist on the Prowl   45
9 | Whatcha Up To? *   47
10 | Biblio Peggy Solo   49
    Duo *   50
11 | Dreams Will Weave   52
12 | That's a Little Sketchy   55
13 | Get Soundtracked   56
14 | It's Your Decision   57
15 | Shutterbug Loveliness   60
16 | Color Me Cured   61
17 | Telepathy Taste Test *   63
18 | I Heard You the First Time *   65
19 | Catchy   68
20 | Sign of the Times   70

PART TWO | TAROT GAMES ... 73

21	A Cross Tick	74
22	Seven Elevens Tarot	76
23	Escape into a Card	77
One	77
Two	78
24	Tarot Spy	79
25	Times are a-Changin' °	80
Note on Change	81
26	You Do You Haiku °	84
Added Option	85
27	One Thing Leads to Another	86
28	Call a Do Over	87
29	What I Truly Want	89
30	Tarot Zoo	90
31	On a Brighter Day	92
Another Option	94
32	Tarot Spy Solitaire	94
33	Awkward Family Tarot	96
A Step Further	101
34	Reverse Tarot	102
35	Lune-a-Day °	103
More Lunes °	104
36	Beside Myself	105
37	Tarot Spy Mission °	106
38	His. Her. Their.	109
First Step	109
39	Art it Up	112
40	The Missing Card	114
First Add-In	114
Second Add-In	116
41	Tarot-for-Two *	118
42	Wheel of Colorful Fortune °	120

Extra Options °	121
43 | Sketchy Too	122
44 | Snapshot	123
45 | Through a Telescope °	125

PART THREE | MEDITATIONS 129

46 | Soundtracked Again	131
47 | Ewe Llama Iguana	132
48 | Up Periscope	133
49 | Like Magic	134
50 | Elementality	136

PART FOUR | APPENDIX..................... 139

Appendix Table of Contents	140
No Peeking Section	**141**
Animal Symbolism Guide	197
Helpful Resources	201
An Afterword	202
About the Author	207
Art Prints	207
Notes	208

* Activities marked with an asterisk are games and activities created especially for two people to try together.

° If marked with this symbol in the table, the activity may work with certain oracle decks, not only tarot.

INDEX of ACTIVITIES

Advice, Answers, Information, Insight, Guidance, Messages
  Beside Myself 105
  Biblio Mania 42
  Biblio Peggy Solo 49
  Biblio Takeaway 32
  Catchy 68
  Color Me Cured 61
  Dreams Will Weave 52
  Elementality 136
  Escape into a Card, Two 78
  Get Soundtracked 56
  His. Her. Their. 109
  I Get It 39
  I Get It, You Can, Too 40
  It's Your Decision 57
  Like Magic 134
  On a Brighter Day 92
  One Thing Leads to Another 86
  Sign of the Times 70
  Sketchy Too 122
  Snapshot 123
  Tarot-for-Two 118
  Tarot Spy 79
  Tarot Spy Mission 106
  Tarot Spy Solitaire 94
  Tarot Zoo 90
  That's a Little Sketchy 55
  Up Periscope 133
  What I Truly Want 89
  Wheel of Colorful Fortune 120

  Word-Fill to Find Insight 37

Affirmations
  Color Me Cured 61
  Escape into a Card 77
  Sketchy Too 122
  What I Truly Want 89
  Wish in the Wind 44
  Word-Fill to Find Insight 37

Animals
  Ewe Llama Iguana 132
  Sign of the Times 70
  Sketchy Too 122
  Tarot Spy 79
  Tarot Zoo 90
  That's a Little Sketchy 55

Balance, Calm, Rest
  Ewe Llama Iguana 132
  Color Me Cured 61
  Sign of the Times 70
  Skip It 31
  Up Periscope 133
  Word-Fill to Find Insight 37

Bibliomancy, Rhapsodomancy
  Biblio Mania 42
  Biblio Peggy Solo 49
  Biblio Takeaway 32
  Catchy 68
  Get Soundtracked 56
  Soundtracked Again 131

Choices, Decisions
  It's Your Decision 57

8

Times are a-Changin' 80

Closure, Resolution
Dreams Will Weave 52
Free and Clear 33

Creativity, Artistic, Sketching
A Cross Tick 74
Art it Up 112
Call a Do Over 87
Lune-a-Day 103
The Missing Card 114
Photojournalist on the Prowl 45
Reverse Tarot 102
Shutterbug Loveliness 60
Sketchy Too 122
Snapshot 123
That's a Little Sketchy 55
You Do You Haiku 84

Dreams/Dreamwork
Dreams Will Weave 52

Exploration, Discovery
Dreams Will Weave 52
Elementality 136
Escape into a Card 77
Ewe Llama Iguana 132
I Heard You the First Time 65
Like Magic 134
Telepathy Taste Test 63
Whatcha Up To? 47

Family
Awkward Family Tarot 96
Color Me Cured 61
Like Magic 134
Snapshot 123

Fears, Overcoming
Free and Clear 33

Future
His. Her. Their. 109
One Thing Leads to Another 86
Snapshot 123
Tarot Spy Mission 106

Games
I Heard You the First Time 65
Sketchy Too 122
Tarot Zoo 90
Telepathy Taste Test 63
That's a Little Sketchy 55
Whatcha Up To? 47
Word-Fill to Find Insight 37

Healing
Beside Myself 105
Color Me Cured 61
Dreams Will Weave 52
Free and Clear 33
On a Brighter Day 92
Skip It 31
Tarot Zoo 90
That's a Little Sketchy 55

Help
On a Brighter Day 92
Times are a Changin' 80

Life Purpose
Times are a-Changin' 80

Manifesting
Escape into a Card 77
Like Magic 134
What I Truly Want 89

Wish in the Wind 44

Meditation

Beside Myself 105

Elementality 136

Escape into a Card 77

Ewe Llama Iguana 132

It's Your Decision 57

Like Magic 134

Sountracked Again 131

Up Periscope 133

What I Truly Want 89

Message of the Day

Biblio Mania 42

Biblio Peggy Solo 49

Biblio Takeaway 32

Get Soundtracked 56

Lune-a-Day 103

Photojournalist on the Prowl 45

Reverse Tarot 102

Seven Elevens Tarot 76

Wheel of Colorful Fortune 120

Music

Art it Up 112

Catchy 68

Get Soundtracked 56

Soundtracked Again 131

Nature/Outdoors

Skip It 31

Wish in the Wind 44

Opportunities

It's Your Decision 57

Tarot Spy Solitaire 94

What I Truly Want 89

Oracle Cards

Lune-a-Day 103

Tarot Spy Mission 106

Through a Telescope 125

Times are a-Changin' 80

You Do You Haiku 84

Wheel of Colorful Fortune 120

Partner/Distance Activity

Biblio Mania 42

Biblio Peggy Solo (Duo) 50

I Get It; You Can, Too 40

I Heard You the First Time 65

Tarot-for-Two 128

Telepathy Taste Test 63

Whatcha Up To? 47

Past

Call a Do Over 87

One Thing Leads to Another 86

Snapshot 123

Perspective

Elementality 136

I Get It 39

Like Magic 134

Snapshot 123

Sketchy Too 122

That's a Little Sketchy 55

Up Periscope 133

What I Truly Want 89

Wheel of Colorful Fortune 120

Photography/Camera

Photojournalist on the Prowl 45

Reverse Tarot 102

Shutterbug Loveliness 60

Snapshot 123

Playing Cards

Beside Myself 105

Poetry

A Cross Tick 74

Art it Up 112

Lune-a-Day 103

You Do You Haiku 84

Relationships, Love, Soul Agreements

His. Her. Their. 109

Sketchy Too 122

That's a Little Sketchy 55

Signs

Dreams Will Weave 52

Sign of the Times 70

Spiritual & Personal Growth, Higher Awareness, Wisdom

Elementality 136

Like Magic 134

Shutterbug Loveliness 60

Sketchy Too 122

Tarot Spy Mission 106

Through a Telescope 125

Wheel of Colorful Fortune 120

Tarot Cards

*See the Tarot Games Section

Like Magic 134

Elementality 136

Tarot Cards – Acquainting

A Cross Tick 74

Awkward Family Tarot 96

Call a Do Over 87

Escape into a Card, One 77

Reverse Tarot 102

Seven Elevens Tarot 76

The Missing Card 114

Lune-a-Day 103

Tarot Spy Mission 106

Tarot Zoo 90

You Do You Haiku 84

Tarot Readings – Personal

Art it Up 112

Elementality 136

Like Magic 134

One Thing Leads to Another 86

Sketchy Too 122

Snapshot 123

Tarot Spy 79

Through a Telescope 125

Times are a Changin' 80

Wheel of Colorful Fortune 120

Tarot Readings – With Friend

Tarot-for-Two 118

Telepathy

I Heard You the First Time 65

Telepathy Taste Test 63

Whatcha Up To? 47

Understanding

Like Magic 134

Sketchy Too 122

Work, Job, Career

Reverse Tarot 102

That's a Little Sketchy 55

Times are a Changin' 80

Up Periscope 133

🦋 **For Kai & Eli**

Congratulations! The world is now your oyster.

All I could do was write you a book.

Introduction

April 27. Four a.m. I am not sure what startled me, but there I was, unable to get back to sleep. It was quiet and still dark. Rolled over, pulled the covers over my head, and hoped for the best. Nope. A half-hour spent reading a photography book until my eyes stopped focusing, lapsed into another thirty minutes of tossing and turning. Until I asked, "Why am I awake?" Within seconds, ideas of games, activities, and meditations started pouring into my head. The sky was trying to help me see, so I grabbed paper and a pen from the basket and started writing. (P.S. If you want to improve your dream recall, keep supplies nearby for mid-night notes, which we will come back to in the activities.) My higher self and spirit guides decided it was a fine time to clock me in.

At 11:22 a.m., I started typing from the notes. There was a pile of loose-leaf papers with notes, instructions, and sketches in disarray next to me. It was a labyrinth of aqua gel-pen scribbling; I hoped I could navigate my way through transcribing.

The wish is for the exercises to bring you a little piece of whatever you might want or need in the moment. New perspective, hope, or plain old fun. This book is an unconventional resource to get to know your cards, acting as an entertaining supplement to traditional tarot studies and spiritual development. A wonderful collection of possibility awaits.

GET it TOGETHER LIST

In using this book, a few supplies are needed for the activities. From the title, obviously, a tarot deck is useful, or several tarot decks to choose from, should you fancy. If you have them already, perfect. If you do not, get your hands on one decent deck to practice with, that is enough. In the event you have never used a tarot deck before, invest in one you genuinely like. Be advised, though. Do not go broke over buying tarot cards. I am not sure what it is, whether it is those first, crisp, shuffling snaps of a fresh deck or mesmerizing artwork, but there are a lot of people who think they will get one deck, you know, "just to see what it is about." Next thing, they have a habit. Whether they learn how to use the cards or not is a separate story.

When you find your deck, protect it. It is a tool that will attune to your personal energy and work better as it does. That means keeping it where others will not handle

INTRODUCTION

it. Storing your cards in a special bag or box is ideal. Wrapping them in a cloth that doubles as a surface covering when you lay out your cards is a smart choice, too.

An old acquaintance once had a collection of thirty-five decks. You can approximate the math on her investment. Over the years she would purchase tarot whenever she noticed artwork she liked, or decks that were unique or collectible. She always kept them up on a shelf, separate from another two that she used regularly.

One night she went to work and left her mother home watching her three-year-old daughter. I recall her contacting me in tears when she returned. All her mother had to say for herself was, "What? She said they were pretty so I let her play with them."

In the bathtub.

Every deck but for one, which she kept safely wrapped in a drawer, was strewn around the house; cards bent, torn, sodden, destroyed.

Please, keep your decks to yourself. Even if you are practicing with a friend, no one should touch them but you. To avoid a case like the woman with the destroyed decks, people in general do not need to know you own them. That way you will not be subject to someone else's unresolved spirituality issues which have nothing to do with you. Having cards should not be about others anyway. They are a personal tool, above all else.

Whether you are a tarot aficionado, a divination queen, or you are breaking open the cellophane seal of your very first deck, jump in. Activities in the book are endeavors and resources in the nature of self-realization. The bulk of the exercises are devised for the individual, to use your tarot deck on your own. In effect, it breaks from certain limitations of standardized methods, yet still upholding the objective to progress self-awareness. The manner of practice does not involve intensive study or memorization. It requires little to no formal knowledge of tarot, nor the necessity to work with spirit guides. That decision is up to each person. Metaphysical curiosity is favored instead. Learn as you go.

For several of the tarot activities, some types of *oracle decks* may work in place of a tarot deck and those games will be noted. However, oracle decks vary tremendously, so decide for yourself based on your cards if a deck is suitable for getting results or not.

In case you are not sure of the difference between tarot and oracle styles, they may discern in the title. A tarot deck consists of 78 cards. They have a base set of twenty-two cards called major arcana, paired with a second set of fifty-six cards broken into four suits. Originated from standard playing cards, the minor arcana combines pip (numerical) cards and court cards.

The term *oracle cards* blankets all other decks that do not fit the tarot structure, such as angel or affirmation cards. To try to appeal to anyone who thinks there is danger or sorcery in coated cardstock, the word *oracle* may be left out of the title. Conversely, there are a handful of oracle decks falsely titled as tarot. A quick investigation online will help in purchasing what you are looking for. There are both amazing and poor options in either genre.

With oracles, the arbitrary quantity of cards in a deck is typically determined by print company stipulations, compared to tarot with its historical origins. Oracle decks began as an artist's stray from the formality of tarot, with designers constructing their own card traits and meanings. These decks now range from those derived from tarot, to conceptually inspired cards, to trivial ones that depict

INTRODUCTION

nothing other than a word or phrase on a flat, single-color background. Pricey lipstick on a pig.

The main point to be aware of with oracles of all types is that lackluster ones are a mere vehicle to drive the user to read generic messages. The person is forced to make those fit to their situations and it ends there. That is fine for those who only want to be told. If you want to cultivate self-awareness and sensory abilities, however, seek out meticulous tarot and oracle decks. Ones the artists have taken care to invest in symbology and detail-rich imagery. Creators of these decks expect people will hold traditional meanings as a foundation, while leaving freedom for personalized, intuitive interpretation. Genuine tarot and oracle decks are a platform for developing your inner voice.

If you are uncertain after looking into your options, a salesperson at a metaphysical bookstore would be able to explain variations to guarantee you find a deck that is well-conceived, artistic, and useful. Browse the suggestions that follow to narrow down options. In the end, always select a deck you are drawn to and that you adore the artwork of, as it motivates inclination to use it. It is also the first sign of a connection between you and the deck.

Use your cards enough and validation arises, proving that you chose the right deck and that self-awareness is growing. A little-known secret about truly marvelous decks? When you have one, no matter how many years you own it or how worn it becomes from use, you will always notice surprising attributes about them. A whole card may even turn up in a new way that makes you wonder how it has been in the deck the entire time. It is evidence that your perception is being honed as you evolve to naturally differentiate each instance of a card through your inner voice, instead of relying on imposed meanings.

Supply List

A notebook, journal, or paper
A pen or pencil
A tarot deck
A few common items which are collected in/
around the home (listed in individual activities)
Optional:
A digital or cell phone camera (for certain activities)

TAROT DECK SUGGESTIONS

In selecting your deck, pay attention to whether it has colorful and detailed artwork throughout, including both the major and the minor (suit) cards. For maximized results with the activities, this will be important. If you only have access to a deck that has elaborate major arcana cards with plain minor arcana cards, separate out the major cards and use them independently for the symbolism activities. *Plain* are those cards showing the coins, wands, swords, and cups with no background imagery. These are decks best left to seasoned users.

Lists that follow are primarily for those who have no idea where to begin looking for a deck. There are hundreds of options out there. Those listed below are altogether appropriate starter decks for anyone interested in learning about tarot, and they all work with this book. Author names are excluded if they are redundant to the title.

INTRODUCTION

Standard & Non-Traditional Tarot Decks (Best)

Chrysalis Tarot, Sierra and Brooks
Connolly Tarot
Everyday Witch Tarot, Alba and Blake
The Goddess Tarot, Kris Waldherr
Hanson-Roberts Tarot
Light Seer's Tarot, Chris-Anne
The New Palladini Tarot
Morgan-Greer Tarot
Old English Tarot, Maggie Kneen
Shadowscapes Tarot, Stephanie Pui-Mun Law
Sharman-Caselli Tarot
Smith-Waite Tarot
Spiritsong Tarot, Paulina Cassidy
Tarot of the Golden Wheel, Mila Losenko
Tarot of a Moon Garden, Karen Marie Sweikhardt
Osho Zen Tarot, Ma Deva Padma
Wildwood Tarot, Ryan, Matthews, and Worthington

Standard & Non-Traditional Decks (Also Good)

Bohemian Gothic Tarot, Ukolov and Mahony
The Good Tarot, Baron-Reid and DelaGrottaglia
Forest of Enchantment Tarot, Weatherstone and Allwood
Haindl Tarot
John Bauer Tarot
Spiral Tarot, Kay Steventon
Rider-Waite Tarot
Thelema Tarot, Lo Scarabeo
Universal Waite, Waite and Hanson-Roberts

There are plenty of activities in the first section to keep you busy until you have found your deck though; tarot games constitute but half the fun.

Marked with an asterisk in the Table of Contents, several opportunities throughout the book are intended for you to work on with a friend. It is essential because a telepathy game on your own amounts to crickets. To make them practicable, they are designed for a distance, over the phone or a video chat. On condition that judgment and expectation are left out of it, they are entertaining for both people. The bonus is bonding and collaborating with each other through the shared experiences.

To assist those who are newer to some of the concepts, metaphysical terminology is defined and offset in italics at the end of exercise the first time it is mentioned.

PRE-TAROT GAMES

While the activities throughout the book do not have any pre-requisites, the Tarot Games section does contain a range between familiarization exercises to personal readings. Although they are designed for people of all abilities, there may be those would like a refresher or new users who want to feel more assured before trying an activity straight out of the box. If that is the case, try the starter worksheets that follow as an introduction to your deck before you move into the Tarot Games section. It oversimplifies your deck but provides a chance to look through all your cards so they will not be completely foreign. More importantly, it gives a foundation from which to launch your own insights. The major and minor arcana are on separate charts. Copy these into your journal for easy referencing. Rather than divided in two as shown, include all four minor suits on one page, if possible.

INTRODUCTION

MAJOR ARCANA WORKSHEET

Look at each card as you fill in the names and a couple main keywords, using the deck's guidebook for assistance. There are many possibilities. As you review, decide on a word the card represents which is meaningful to *you*. They are your cards; if you connect through a word association unique to you, trust this. Use these keywords as a mental starting point if ever stuck on a meaning. Acquaintance exercises will further nurture understanding of your cards.

	CARD NAME	KEYWORDS UPRIGHT | REVERSED
0		
I		
II		
III		
IV		
V		

VI		
VII		
VIII		
IX		
X		
XI		
XII		
XIII		
XIV		
XV		
XVI		

INTRODUCTION

XVII		
XVIII		
XIX		
XX		
XXI		

MINOR ARCANA WORKSHEET

Once you fill in the keywords, the chart may be read to include the key for all suits plus your keyword. If you put the word *partnership* in the Two of Wands space, it could be thought of as "balance of partnership." A second example is if you assigned *generosity* for the Queen of Wands, it could be read as "growth of generosity" or it could signify a person with a developed nature of generosity. Include card reversal keywords if you wish.

Change words in gray to match your deck if needed.

	Keys of All Suits	WANDS spirit/work	CUPS emotions/love
ACE	beginnings		
2	balance		
3	creation		
4	foundation		
5	challenges		
6	harmony		
7	potential		
8	progress		
9	final stage		
10	completion		
PAGE	messengers of:		
KNIGHT	action of:		
QUEEN	growth /of:		
KING	authority or decisions of:		

INTRODUCTION

	Keys of All Suits	SWORDS knowledge	PENTACLES power/finances
ACE	beginnings		
2	balance		
3	creation		
4	foundation		
5	challenges		
6	harmony		
7	potential		
8	progress		
9	final stage		
10	completion		
PAGE	messengers of:		
KNIGHT	action of:		
QUEEN	growth of:		
KING	authority or decisions of:		

PART ONE
AWARENESS ACTIVITIES

WITHIN THIS SECTION OF THE BOOK ARE EXERCISES AND games to try on your own. They are intended for diversion and revealing facets of yourself. Try not to take the results stringently. Do not run off with gypsies or make shocking, life-altering decisions based on them. But do savor the discoveries. Used correctly, with pure intention, they have the potential to help you understand how you perceive information, and how to connect at a higher level of awareness with your true, innermost self.

You can do the activities throughout the book in any order you are drawn to do so. They have a variety of purposes which are found in the Index of Activities on page 8. Having a journal or notebook dedicated to use with this book is helpful, especially when you repeat an exercise and compare your results. Hang on to the notes as it is fascinating to reflect on after some time passes. You are sure to see how much progress you make.

ACTIVITY WARM-UP

Promote impressive results in working with this book, by having a little ritual to begin activities. It sets the tone and puts the mind in a self-aware space. The habit of it is like plugging your energy into source energy current.

For those who are already practicing it, a grounding, cleansing, and protection visualization is recommended. Feel free to keep up with doing so here. No sense in disrupting what works. For anyone who wants to go to that extent, there are complete how-to instructions in *Through the Blue Door: A Medium's Guide to Ultra-Sensory Meditation and Journaling.* As an alternative for now, here is a simple routine to try.

Either standing or sitting, stretch your arms straight up over your head and rotate your wrists. If you are unable, that is not an issue; modify this to what is physically comfortable for you. Look up and see your body and energy stretching up high. Imagine streamers of white light wrap around your wrists as you twirl them. Then, as you bring your hands back down to your sides, envision the streamers of light twist and swirl all down around you, protecting you in this higher vibration of pure energy. As you finish, exclaim, "Let's do this!" or use an equivalent pep rally rouser. And, just like that, you are ready to go.

AWARENESS ACTIVITIES

SKIP IT: An Activity for Calm

For this emotional and mental healing exercise, there are both outdoor and indoor versions to practice. Do what suits you depending on the day. They can be done as often as it interests you but trust that you will know which is the best fit for your personal circumstances each time.

If Outdoors

Find a small stone. As you hold on to it, imagine that unwanted energy within you will be transferred into the rock. Excess energy that is causing you distress or imbalance in any way. Think to yourself, "Little Stone, please do me the favor of carrying away my _____ (upset, sadness, anxiety, stress, anger, unwanted energy, etc.) and allow the Air to bring me peace." When you feel that you have finished releasing the energy, toss the rock to a place nearby where it will be hidden, remaining undisturbed until a rain cleanses it. Preferably, skip the stone into a nearby body of water if that is an option. Close your eyes and feel the air against your skin with each breath in and out. Stay this way a moment, inviting the calmness of Earth energy to wash over you. Become aware of your presence in that moment. Feel yourself aligned to your surroundings. Nature is here to heal us and is especially effective when we work in partnership, allowing for it to happen.

If Indoors

In place of an actual stone, use one precious square of toilet paper crumpled into a ball, which will act as your "rock." Use the same process and saying as above but skip it into the toilet and let it be flushed away from you forever. In this instance too, you should close your eyes and feel the air around you. If you have an adjacent room with a ceiling fan running that you can step into, or an open window to stand by; feel the wave of equilibrium take effect. Concentrate on the air bringing you peace. If you are at work or school, this is at least expedient.

It may not feel as ceremonial standing around the porcelain bowl as compared to Lake Winnibigoshish and the pine forest, but nevertheless it involves nature-based elements that work in a pinch.

As an alternative, you could try the same routine while in the shower. Though not entirely an earth element, pretend a dollop of shampoo or body wash is your stone, drawing excess energy away from you as you hold it in the palm of your hand. Let it suds up and rinse down the drain, as the running water and air restore you.

BIBLIO TAKEAWAY

Speediest activity in the book. This is the fast-food drive-through of insight. Think to yourself, "What do I need to hear right now?"

Grab the first book that catches your eye and without looking, flip it open to a page, any page. Eyes closed, run your finger slowly down that page until you feel you ought to stop. Read the sentence you land on. If you have an inkling you need the entire paragraph or remainder of the chapter, continue reading. Oftentimes one sentence is all that is needed to convey the key message.

On occasion the sentence is clearly out of humor and splashes levity into your day. Other times, it relates to a life situation. Still other times it does not make sense up front but turns out to be a precursor to an event days later that explains.

Record the sentence in your journal.

It is optional to spend time pondering and writing about this and the significance either right away, or when you are winding down for the day.

Congratulations. You accomplished a divination. The simplest of kinds. Easy. Accessible. Works in all sorts of situations and takes little time investment. Yet, you tend to learn what you need to in the moment.

Virtual high-five if you caught the *biblioteca* pun.

Bibliomancy: Divination by opening a book to a random page and reading a passage. The prefix biblio- *specifically implicates the origin of the custom, using a bible for this purpose.*

Divination: The practice of acquiring information about past, present, or future by ultra-sensory means and/or by using tools of divination, such as tarot, rune stones, and I Ching.

Ultra-senses: Senses perceived beyond the range or limits of ordinary, moderate physical sensory perception; sensory perception at a higher frequency than common human experience.

FREE and CLEAR

This is a simple, thoughtful journaling activity for addressing emotional healing. The idea behind it is to connect a material item with the intangible idea of overcoming an issue, breaking a cycle, keeping on track with your personal freedom, or preventing a blockage to your next momentous happening.

The hardest part of the activity may be the preparation, which is going into your closet or through a drawer, or your purse, backpack, or briefcase to find an article you no longer need. It might be time for it to move on to a new home via a donation box. Or, it could be an item that is used up or no longer serving a purpose. It is in no way intended to part with anything near and dear to your heart. The activity is about finding one personal item, small or large, which by your free will you are ready to be rid of, in conjunction with clearing an emotional sticky spot.

And yes, the item needs to be one of your own. No using this as excuse to chuck out a loved one's oddball collection. Not even her eroded, end-of-the-school-year leggings. Yeah, you know the ones. Maybe replace those tomorrow.

Again, look for one single item. Going full Marie Kondo for this is not the goal. Keep it simple. At least until you decide to repeat the exercise another day and select an entirely different piece.

Now once you have your item and properly part with it, settle in a comfortable spot for a few minutes of journaling. The objective is to think about how this object that stood out to you today represents a facet of your life. In getting rid of it, it allows you to unburden yourself in some way. Choose what you are ready to change. It is likely an upset you have been working on overcoming anyway. The odds are that putting in this last bit of intentional thought-processing brings a final resolution. If it is an entirely new matter you want to work through, that is perfectly fine as well.

With regard to the healing, the item may be symbolic due to its condition, size, color, or the purpose it served. It could be a representation of memories associated with it. But think of the object and parallel that with an emotional aspect to clear within yourself.

Address questions such as, how does freeing yourself of the object and outmoded beliefs or burdensome feelings lift you up? What did you learn from it in the past? Which part of the human experience did it exemplify? What is it you can let go of? How does that open room in your heart and mind for you? What is a new factor that might fill that space? How would you describe the freedom that comes from putting an agony to rest?

If you are stumped, try this method of breaking down the item description in the left-hand column (see diagram). These are the symbols; complete this side first.

In the right-hand column, write what each descriptive word symbolizes to you. It parallels what you are freeing yourself from concerning that life situation.

Go back to those questions in the previous paragraph afterwards to write free flowing thoughts about it below the diagram.

At the bottom of your page, when finished with the columns and journaling, add one extra part. Write these last sentences so you always remember, "I have awareness of what this is, and I do not need it to be an ongoing part of my life experience any longer. I am now free to be my true, soul self." Complete the sentence, "In getting rid of _____, I also get rid of _____ and heal _____. This makes me free and clear to fill my life with the _____ I want instead."

Diagram:

ITEM: _____	LIFE SITUATION: _____
Descriptive Words:	**Description Symbolizes:**
1.	
2.	
3.	
…up to	
10.	

Example:

ITEM: Stuffed Animal	LIFE SITUATION:
Descriptive Words:	**Description Symbolizes:**
Black	fear, worry, false thoughts
Fuzzy	static, friction, but not dangerous or damaging
Cute (personified, but if it were real, it would be unsafe)	things are not always what they seem; be cautious in trusting depending on the version
Received as a gift	what someone else had to offer; is not a reflection of me, is not my choice
A representation of a real living being	that I deserve what is real and true; do not deserve a wolf in sheep's clothing

AWARENESS ACTIVITIES

WORD-FILL to FIND INSIGHT

Complete the word-fill as a first step to this divine guidance activity. You may copy it into a journal page or find the free PDF at https://MandorlaAcademy.com/shop to download and print, listed as *In the Moment.*

Go in a random order with the words from the list; if it is done as shown, the results will not be as useful.

Each time you write an answer, sequentially number the word you placed, as the order has significance later.

Upon completion, forward to the No Peeking section (page 194) to check answers and gather your results. Any word that is skipped or incorrectly used in the puzzle is to be excluded from the interpretation portion.

Words to Fit

- abundance
- adventure
- balance
- celebration
- connection
- exercise
- explore
- family
- fulfillment
- friends
- gratitude
- happy
- healthy
- hobby
- hope
- home
- learn
- love
- passion
- peace
- purpose
- resilience
- security
- sharing
- success
- trust
- truthful

IN the MOMENT WORD-FILL PUZZLE

I GET IT

Before starting this insight activity, decide on a question you want to ask, surrounding whatever has been on your mind as of late. Word this as open-ended, not as a yes or no question. Set the intention it to be answered by writing it at the top of your journaling page.

Next, go to either your kitchen utensils drawer or toolbox and open it. Close your eyes and hover your hand above it, a few inches away in a slow motion. When you feel you should stop over a certain item, do so and point your finger down at it. Open your eyes. Take that item with you to look at as you continue journaling.

For the subsequent part, describe the item you found. Do not worry about your question yet. Take care of the descriptive parts first. Below your question write these sentence starters and complete them.

The item is a:
It looks (color, size, shape):

It is made of:

It feels (texture, temperature, weight):

It also:
(Here describe other features; if it makes a sound, if it has moving parts, if it has a scent, if it has several components or is singular/solid, etc.)

It is typically used for:

It makes me think of:

Now look back over what you have written, as a whole. From those words, write a paragraph that interprets the symbolism as an answer to your question. Taking into account various ways to view a situation, this process bares an honest answer or a perspective you had not considered. At a minimum it provides extra pieces to the puzzle you are trying to work through.

I GET IT; YOU CAN, TOO

This is the version of I Get It to enjoy with a friend over the phone or video chat. It is a *household divination* exercise we have practiced over the years in one of my workshops. In fact, I have an oval box of items expressly collected for it. Students select from this trove of oddities without having to blindly reach into my real junk drawer and risk getting stuck with a pin. It also eliminates having to endure ten different fridge magnet interpretations. We have done variants of this activity at different times and I am including a few here. Discuss between yourselves which style you want to try.

In each instance, offer the description and the symbolism, along with your explanation, as insight to the friend's question. This is different than in the solo version where you evaluate for yourself. The variations are:

Option 1: Choose the first item you see on the desk you are sitting at (or within arm's reach).

Option 2: Assign each other a room in your home from which to choose an object – what first catches your eye

AWARENESS ACTIVITIES

– run back to where you were first sitting and continue the exercise. Set a timer for a ridiculous pace if you want to give it a parkour flair, or, if you have a friend who is easily distracted and might not get back to you. If your friend is a second-guesser, for sure set the timer. (Finding an object should take about five seconds, tacking on time to get to the room and back fairly).

Option 3: Dig through your purse or backpack for the item.

Option 4: Run to your car to choose. Who knows what symbolism a stray, stale French fry might bear?

Option 5: Come up with four separate questions each, making a marathon of taking turns to share personal symbolism and thoughts. Use all the options above, once per person.

The easiest way to go about this is for the *interpreter* to detail the object's symbolism to start. The other person then reveals their question. Going back to the interpreter, who finishes with a well-rounded summary that answers the question. This is abbreviated, but a conversation may go like this:

"I am looking at the snow globe I picked up and it is a miniature world of its own for the snowman inside. Self-contained. The snowman is smiling. There is snow, but it feels cozy like being at home by the fireplace in winter, rather than cold outside. I think that is it. What question did you ask?" (There is usually a natural pause, so you do not need to push to keep elaborating).

"My question was, 'Is it in my best interest to accept the job offer to work from home instead of at the office?'"

"Based on what the symbolism meant to me this time, I think that the answer is yes. It felt like being indoors at home and cozy, as in safe and secure. You would not feel left out in the cold or separated by not being active in the office setting."

Make it light and simple. It does not have to be elaborate and it should not feel like you are making up the meanings, forcing a description to answer a question. The ideas should flow easily, if briefly. In an instance where you draw a blank, that is fine. Try another question or take a break and come back to it after a few minutes. It is meant for enjoyment, not life and death decisions anyway.

BIBLIO MANIA

Hurry to get your message-of-the-day. Choose the fourth book nearest you. Open to page 106 and read the seventh sentence.

This is one further twist on bibliomancy, having a predetermined route to your sentence and hopefully, a useful message. The happenstance technique of opening to a random page to find your passage is favored, as in Biblio Takeaway, because we tend to do this when a book catches our eye and makes us think to crack it open. It is also based on one's own energetic influence, instead of someone else's directive. It is relevant to put different approaches to the test, though, as both can work.

If you want to try this method again, pick up a book and ask another person to give you two numbers from sets, such as between 1-300 for the page number, and 1-15 for the sentence. Should you be at a café or in the airport and you ask the guy next to you for your numbers, who knows, it could be your meet-cute. They may want to try it, too.

It is also appealing to go a little bibliomaniac. Put together an eclectic collection, say at least ten books of various subjects and genres shelved together, to offer astute advice when the bibliomancy mood strikes. Poetry, classic and modern fiction, non-fiction, self-help. Any book may work. Try to keep the overall illustration content to a lower percentage. If it happens that you try to get a message and you land on a diagram or a picture, while there may be advice within that, it can be a disappointment when you are hoping for clearer reassurance of actual words. However, I must say, a friend and I did this exercise together and his book ended up being a Linux manual. I had laughed thinking there was no way it would work, but the single sentence directly answered our question. The lesson in *do not judge a book by its cover* was included as a bonus.

Technically, I should add here that using a poetry book is called *rhapsodomancy*, divination by means of verse. Stick that in your brain for trivia night and you will not get docked a point for calling it bibliomancy.

Back to the message you received. Feel free to write it down and spend a little time journaling. If it made sense immediately, you may want to spell out the whole story, so future-you appreciates what you were writing about. If it confused you or did not make sense whatsoever, that does not mean clarification is not going to follow along shortly. Record it as, "This was my message for the day; I do not know what it means yet." You can always return to it and update the entry. When the Universe is trying to connect with us, it will not stop trying to bridge our understanding.

WISH in the WIND: Activity for Hope

Here is a quick practice for a windy day where you can step outside even if for a couple minutes. The windier the better. If you try on a still day, you might be standing there for quite a long time. Quite. A. Long. Time.

Now, this is leans on being an exercise in magic and manifesting over anything. If you say it cannot work, then stop here because it will not; you already decided. On the other hand, if you believe miracles happen, that is another story. This is made for you. Understand that all it may take for change to come is setting the intention and carrying the will to allow blessings. That is the key.

To prepare for this you need three leaves. These can be leaves you find on the ground, or three blades of grass, or else bay leaves from your kitchen herbs collection.

Once you have the leaves in hand, mull over how you want to restore hopefulness. What area or situation in life needs a lift? As you have that in mind, come up with three options or aspects you wish to manifest, change, or grow to improve this part of your life.

Assign one wish to each leaf. If you want to write on the leaves or mark them so you know which is which, that is helpful. Once the wishes are clear, set all three leaves on the ground in a row in front of you at the same time. If you have difficulty to bend down to do this, lay them flat in a row in the palm of your hand instead, which you extend out into the wind. If you are seated, they can be laid across your lap or on a picnic table.

Pay attention to the last leaf that blows away. This part of the wish is thought to be the first to come true. Once the leaves are carried away by the wind, use this affirmation to conclude your hopeful mission:

> "My wishes have been carried by the wind into the world. Now it is up to my soul and divine timing to carry the blessings back to me."

Close your eyes for a second to feel the constructive energy at work before you pop back inside to warm up.

Affirmation: A precise declaration of what you believe, desire, or imagine your life to be, with intention toward manifesting the aspect into being.

Manifest: Bringing dreams and desires to reality by applying creative thought and dynamic energy through any number of means, often spiritually based.

PHOTOJOURNALIST on the PROWL

This is a message-for-the-week exercise. You will need your cell phone camera or a regular digital camera for this. None available? No problem. Take mental snapshots with your hands held out to make a finger frame and write descriptive notes.

For this practice take five separate photos around your home. An idea is to take one picture per room. A second idea is to photograph one feature along each wall of a single room, plus one extra, perhaps of an item on the floor. This is where the prowl comes in, before you start shooting your photos, take a walk around and see what feels right to you. There is no wrong way to go about it, so follow your instinct to get results.

When you are ready to take your pictures, attempt to do this from a close-up position, emphasizing one or two objects as focal points in the picture. A set of pieces may count as one. Try not to move anything if possible; take the picture of the scene as-is. It is alright if there are background components to the picture, or secondary elements, even if they are partially cropped out of the view.

If you try to take a picture of a whole room, the exercise will not bring a depth of insight. Confusion, maybe. So, think of it like this. The scope of the answer is in correlation to the range of what you photograph. If you want a distinct outcome, the photograph should not be broad. That being said, no one need look at life under a microscope, so macrophotography is not ideal in this situation either. Nonetheless, if a hypercritical moment struck and you insist on macros, that is up to you, but it is not the plan for the activity.

Do not worry about perfection in your pictures. Go with one shot of each scene if possible. They can be deleted once you are finished anyway.

When you have all five photos, you are ready for the next part and can jump to the Appendix No Peeking Section, page 149.

WHATCHA UP TO?

For this activity you need a cohort going in on it with you. Ideally this is someone not living with you. An accomplice fully up for the task you assign them. A BFF. Trustworthy to a fault. Not at all judgy. The one who says, "I am in!" whenever you have an outrageous idea, or in this case, a telepathy experiment to try.

The first objective is deciding on a time frame you want to use for your research. A couple options are presented below, but you should determine this based on how prompt you both can be with your part. It entirely depends on how your schedules align.

> Option 1: A one-day experiment, with four or five times pre-determined throughout the day and spread out. For example, Wednesday at 10 a.m., 1 p.m., 4 p.m. and 7 p.m.; allowing five minutes each time.

> Option 2: A one-week experiment, with one time pre-determined per day for seven days. Sunday through Saturday at noon; allowing three minutes per time, for instance.

Both people have a role. You will be the receiver and your partner will be the sender. It is up to you to decide together if you want to double your experiment time and swap roles. But do not go back and forth taking turns, switch roles upon completion. In using option one, you would be the receiver for one day and then have your partner to be the receiver the second day. For version two, swap roles after one week.

In either case, do not discuss your results until the end of the experiment timeframe. At that point, have a lively conversation about it and deliberate your experiences. Decide during that time if you want to repeat the activity or try a new version of it and see if you get similar or improved results.

The second objective is deciding the two action choices for the sender. At designated times, you as the receiver pay attention to what you think the sender is doing, while the sender does one of the two chosen activities for the duration you decided on. Allowing from one minute to five minutes is suggested. Have your clocks synchronized and alarms set so you do not end up off schedule.

While of course you can think of your own plan, some choices would be eating a snack, talking out loud, singing or humming, dancing, clapping or snapping fingers, walking or jogging, writing or drawing, building with blocks or putting together a puzzle. Try to choose two activities involving two different senses, especially during a first-time trial, rather than choosing two activities that would be similar in a sensory way. For instance, it may be harder for a receiver to tell the difference between writing and doing a puzzle, compared to the difference between eating and jogging.

After your experiment is over, especially if you have taken turns at both roles, talk about what you found easiest or toughest to pick up on mentally. Were there other challenges that made a difference, such as it feeling difficult to tune in to each other at a set time of day? Feel free to mix up the activities and try a new combination if you are having an enjoyable time with it and are up for a second round of conducting tests together.

Two other versions of partner experiments appear in the activities section to try out later. See if you can get successful results here first, as the games increase in difficulty.

BIBLIO PEGGY SOLO

"What if we put two and two together, Peggy?"

"Great question." Let us see how that works, teaming up with someone else to get messages. But first, a solo version of this third style of bibliomancy divination.

Think of a question and begin your journal entry with it. Leave space to add the response and think of a second question on another topic. It can be challenging to come up with questions, but if that happens, think a little outside yourself. Ask about a theme on a community, national, world, or universal level, rather than personal life matters. Such as, "What should I know about _____?" or "What is the significance of _____?" or "How might _____ have an influence on _____?"

Continue by picking out three books. Select any that you like or are drawn to at the time. Be thoughtful about what order they should go in as a stack though. The middle book will be used twice.

As with the earlier method, having your eyes closed, flip to a random page of the first book and run your finger down the page until it feels right to stop. Read that sentence. Record it right away or else keep the page marked so you do not lose it. Try to not analyze or interpret it yet.

Rather, continue, repeating the process with the next book. Once you have the two sentences put together, consider how they combine to give information or clues toward your question. Journal about this if you wish. For sure leave space in case a significant event comes up later bringing validation to record.

For your second question, do the exercise the same way. Use the second book followed by the third to collect two new sentences with intention of them pertaining to your second question.

If you think of a third question to ask as you work through the initial questions, add that to your list. Select one sentence from each of the three books this time. Use those to assemble a unified answer.

DUO

This time engage Peggy (or better, a real-life friend) in a chat and try this exercise together at the same time.

Both of you should think of your own open-ended question and make note of them. Do not share what the questions are yet. Decide who will be the first querent. Unless someone is incensed by the messages or falls asleep on the task, everyone gets a turn.

The querent should choose a color and a number from one to five. Share the choices with the other person. Both people then find the books based on that. The first book is that number on the shelf or stack. The second book is the one you spot with the designated color on the spine or as the main color of the cover.

Once you both have two books in hand, the querent considers their question while the co-pilot thinks, "What is the advice toward _____'s question?"

Use the same method for each book of blindly opening to a random page, extracting a single sentence. The querent should write their two passages on paper first. Then add the friend's two passages to the list. At that point, the querent should reveal their opening question and read the list of sentences aloud.

From there, see how the messages compare. Do the four sentences complement or contradict each other? Can they be combined to give a clearer overall answer to the querent's question? Indulge in a proper discussion on this so the querent comes away with an answer or understanding. If it was an awkward question or response, there is always the option to circumvent and instead talk about the weather before switching turns.

Meanwhile, the biblio-puns are getting worse, I admit. *Bibliopegy*, the binding of books, was irresistible to play off when putting the bibliomancy exercises together. The point being, it is rewarding to mix things up and try variations on divination practices to see what works best for you personally. When the results are synchronistic it is an added boost. Occasionally it seems a jumble, and Peggy is confused. It is still worth the attempt to absorb how it all works. Plus, you never know when an explanation arrives, bringing comprehension to the message.

Over the years, students have brought divination tools along to class asking to be taught how to use them. I would figure them out and encourage my advanced students to test them together. It speeds up the trial and error and is valid feedback having the varied perceptions. Other times I riddled out centuries-old divination methods that have no recorded instruction books existing, as an opportunity for some ultra-sensory investigation. At some point, it led to devising a couple methods of divination of my own. In a roundabout way, I suppose that explains how this book is coming to be. Finding creative slants for cool humans to engage their inner spirits is always a refreshing challenge.

Synchronicity: Divine timing; a sequence of related, meaningful, and remarkable or unexpected events.

DREAMS WILL WEAVE

There are functions to our dreams and our sleep state beyond what is commonly understood. Those who delve into dream interpretation record their dreams in a journal regularly. In doing so, they pay closer attention to the subconscious mind or soul to get to the root of issues for healing and resolution. For some, developing this understanding then becomes a tool for working with their higher self and spirit guides, solely because of being open to it.

If you would like to get started with dreamwork, this activity is for you. It is likewise perfect for those wanting to improve natural occurrences of dream awareness, so they will become less random.

As you are settling into bed for the night, check that you have paper and pencil within reach. Use notebook or loose-leaf paper, so you can transpose any middle of the night scribbles in the dark into a legible journal entry when you are fully awake.

AWARENESS ACTIVITIES

Before you doze off, ask your higher self (by thought or out loud, as you prefer) to connect with you in dream state for one of the following options.

- To receive a single symbol, that if you see it during waking state you will know they are with you.
- To receive advice regarding a situation you are struggling with.
- To receive encouragement and healing.
- To explore a place that you have not traveled to before.

After that, be sure you add, "...and I ask that I be allowed to remember this in the morning."

Should you wake up in the middle of the night with an answer, or aware of what you were dreaming, make a few notes or write key words. It is not necessary to be thorough or to analyze it right then. Put down enough so it aids recall once you are ready to wake up at a decent hour.

To develop dream recall and to put this dreamwork into action, yielding successful results may take a little time. Do not be discouraged if you are without a clear message on the first try. Allow at least a week or two to adapt to the habit. Ask each night. Have a clear question, not asked in desperation or fear. This sets the intention that you are ready to receive an answer.

Of course, not scheduling enough sleep time, disrupted sleep patterns, or other inhibiting factors play a role in getting your dream state to work for you. If you are drawn to it, keep trying and let it weave together. Trial and error are part of the process. It is no different than learning a language, this newly intended means of interaction. Once it is established as a form of communication, the recall, symbolism, messages, and signs all begin to come naturally. Often it is with no effort or asking because you developed this open connection.

As last bits of advice, permit yourself to run with it. Your experience does not have to match anyone else's for it to be legitimate. Pay attention to what brings you desired outcomes. Know that asking about a simpler matter to start out may result in validation to build your confidence. Any symbolism that comes across, remember to apply what it means to you personally before weighing out the traditional ideas.

Higher Self (the Self): A person's soul, the Divine or complete spirit; one's spiritual whole; differentiated from the Earthly human personality and ordinary essence of being.

AWARENESS ACTIVITIES

THAT'S a LITTLE SKETCHY

You can draw a stick figure? Magnificent. This means you are fully qualified for this sketching game.

Before you go add that to your résumé or start the activity, think of a work or relationship question you want to ask and record that at the top of your journal page, with notes and evaluation to follow.

Use a blank page in your journal, an index card, a clean sheet of printer paper, or the blank backside of some junk mail. If you want to draw on a smaller scale use part of the page, but 4x6" should be about the smallest area to use for your drawing. A pen, pencil, marker, or colored pencil are all suitable. Color will not be evaluated for this activity, but perfectly acceptable for your own aesthetic. You never know if a hundred years from now someone comes across it, connects some dots, and claims you were Banksy.

Implement in hand, draw the following list of subjects on your paper. Add them in the order listed but place them in any position in your picture. That is to say, the list is determined, but the artistic liberty is all yours.

> **Subjects**
> A tree
> A tent
> A campfire
> A pond
> A bird

When you have finished your masterpiece, jump to page 184 of the Appendix to evaluate your work.

GET SOUNDTRACKED

Here is another option for getting a worded message for the day or for answering a specific question. Since song lyrics are also verse, this is another adaptation of rhapsodomancy. Only, this method comes straight from your playlist, rather than poetry. For today we will say you are about to get soundtracked.

To start, decide the source of your music. It is necessary to be able to select a track at random so use a device or app with a shuffle feature. The more diverse the music in the collection the better. Any reasonable length playlist should work.

At this point, decide on a question or if you prefer, a general message for the day. Write that down at the top of your journaling page so there is no misunderstanding if you were mulling the options over for a while.

Now, think to yourself, "Self, (to address your soul or higher self) send me a song to give me the assurance I need." Then hit shuffle and play the first song that comes up. Your message may be the song title, the chorus, or a special verse. If you get through the whole song without it making sense, look up the exact lyrics and read them. Seeing them in print lets your eyes be drawn to the applicable part. It can happen that the words you need to find appear to be highlighted or stand out in some way. The message rarely is an entire song because that is a complete story written by another person for their own reasons, and your history will never be identical. Look for that one meaningful phrase, verse, or chorus and do not let other parts of the song detract from it.

As always, log your message and relevant backstory.

IT'S YOUR DECISION

You are faced with a major choice. Weighing out the pros and cons, involved in a tug o' war between head and heart. It is wise to be logical but also to trust your instinct. But then there is that fine line. Skip back and forth across it a few times and it is dizzying. Self-doubt takes hold. Because of that, people end up choosing whatever they deem practical or commonplace, ignoring upset bodily functions as it happens. Choosing based on fear.

Worse still, when faltering results in allowing someone else to make the choice for them instead. No one has access to someone else's soul's life plan. What are the odds they get it right when they have nothing except their own parameters to go by?

If you believe in your inner self, try this *clairsentience* activity to guide or validate your decision-making process.

Before attempting this, it is crucial to put yourself into a wholly peaceful or neutral state. If you are in panic, fear, anxiety, desperation, or upset of any sort, you will not get a response that is reliable. Repeating that because it is that important: *This activity only works if you are calm.*

Find a quiet place to do your activity so you can focus without being disturbed. This begins with having several matching scraps of paper. On each one, write one of the choices. For instance, if you were thinking of moving, you would write the names of towns you are interested in on separate papers.

After you write all the options you are trying to decide between, always add one extra paper in the batch that reads: *an option I have not yet considered*. This is meant to encompass any possibility or opportunity that has not been revealed to you yet. Fold all the scraps and mix them up so you do not know which is which. Set them spaced apart in a row.

Close your eyes for a moment and pay attention to how your energy feels right now. What you want to gauge is how your energy changes when you are in contact with each piece of paper. Begin with the first, holding it in the palm of your weaker hand (not the one you write with). Think to yourself, "Is this option in my absolute interest? How does this option feel?" Determine how your energy shifts. Write a description, including any physical or emotional reaction you may have had to it. Place the paper back in its place in the row though, so you do not get them mixed up. Repeat the process for each paper.

This whole activity can be done in a matter of minutes. Some prefer to be meditative about it, holding a single paper for a short while and others are able to determine within seconds. It is up to you what is needed. Just know that if you are second guessing while holding a paper, you either spent too long on it, or were not in a grounded state at the start.

You do not need to dwell on it, because that is the entire point. Keeping your mind out of it. *Feel* it. Imagine each piece of paper gives you varying degrees of electrical energy. It is a subtlety of current you are paying attention for, one that is a tingly flicker of warmth and happiness, not one that fries your hair to stand on end. Not one that feels weighed down, dense, or heavy, but is light and airy.

Repeat the process of holding the paper scraps individually, making your determination.

Finish going through all options once. If you processed several, compare the two you felt were promising, to determine which comes out ahead.

In the end, open each paper to see the answers and the feelings you associated with them. While this should not *finalize* the decision for you, it may confirm what you already knew in your heart. Or, it may give reason to explore the top option further in order to arrive at your decision. Either way, listening to your inner voice is an effective tool.

A word of caution, however. Be mindful about how you word your questions. If your situation involves other people and you are asking what is in your best interest, the answer you get may not be the same as asking what is valuable to the other person. One example of this, a woman was trying to decide about where to take their family vacation as they had a few options. The way she posed the initial question resulted in her preferred destination being the choice. But asking for which trip would be enjoyed most for the family overall, it brought a different outcome.

If you are asking about a complex matter, then respectfully follow up with meditations on it or do other work to gather as much knowledge as possible.

Clairsentience: The ability to perceive physical and emotional feelings by ultra-sensory means; "clear-feeling." From French, clair *(clear) + Latin,* sentire *(to feel).*

Life Plan: A soul's overall intention for circumstances it wishes to encounter, achieve, and experience during a human lifetime. Life purpose (soul purpose) being part of that, as well as the fulfillment of soul agreements to all others.

SHUTTERBUG LOVELINESS

We have another photography and journaling activity to try. This time you will be taking up to five photos again. Use a cell phone camera or digital camera if you have one, but if not, your trusty finger frame viewer works, too. This time you are welcome to stage your pictures somewhat if you like. Although, symbolism may be found in taking the shot as-is by seeing how the objects you photograph are normally situated. Either way, go about it how it appeals to you.

Now the challenge of the activity is to find up to five meaningful gifts you have received. Material gifts were the plan, but if you are leaning toward an abstract, like the gift of time or forgiveness, then take a photograph that is symbolic of that to you. It is your activity; you can make it work.

Have all your pictures? Then you are ready to move on to the journaling part.

Start by writing a basic label and description for the gift. Follow with an explanation as to why it is a favorite and what it means to you. Next, expand on thoughts of the person who gifted it to you. You might tell the story of how it was gifted. Did you receive it for a special occasion? What does this person mean to you? Are there correlations between the person and the item? Beyond the object, look at the setting, lighting, and how it is used or displayed. What are the symbolic implications in that? Weigh any thoughts that come to mind as you are reflecting on your connection to this person. Let the ideas flow.

When you are about to finish or switch to the next picture, send the person an energy bubble of loving mojo in your thoughts and let their soul know how grateful you are for them. In the next few days, if it is in your heart to do so, connect with them personally for a visit.

Repeat the process for each picture and item. This exercise is for and about you first and foremost. It is aimed at growing self-awareness. This may be in realizing your connection to others, or it may be about gratitude for someone, or heaps of other possibilities. Reflect on this. Think about the ways these people have offered gifts beyond what you photographed and how that influences you today.

> *Loveliness: A group of ladybugs may be referred to as a loveliness. Or in this case, the lovelies in your life, you Shutterbug. And to clarify, actual ladybugs, not their wicked stepsister Asian lady beetles. Groups of those are a nastiness; or that is what they ought to be called.*

COLOR ME CURED

This is an energy exercise directed toward resolving personal need. What might benefit you right now? Our body and soul try to tell us the answer more often than we realize. A simple tool like this helps us listen. Let your subconscious give its assessment. By no means is this a scientific or medically suggestive pursuit. It purely is practice in energetic self-awareness; the "cure" in this case is heightened attention to your needs. It should go without saying, if you need a to see a medical doctor for any reason, then please do so. You matter.

Now the exercise is simple. You need a set of seven matching items in seven separate colors that you hold on to for the activity. The colors required are black, red, orange, yellow, green, blue, and purple. Try to use objects that are identical but for their colors. They should not have multiple colors, unless a second color is on all the items. For example, if you chose to use matching toy cars which are individual, solid colors, but all have black wheels. That is fine.

Possibilities include colored pencils, crayons, markers, squares of paper, magnets, paper clips, buttons, *Legos* (of the same size and shape), marbles, or other small toys.

If you do not find any options around home, use a computer to download the free Color Blocks PDF at www.MandorlaAcademy.com/shop. After color-printing a copy, cut them into individual squares, separate out the seven that you need, and you are all set. Print the document onto an opaque white cardstock paper; the cards can be stored in a small envelope tucked into your journal.

For the exercise, set all seven items in front of you in a row. Handle one at a time, making sure you are not physically in contact with the other items. In any order, pick up each item, without looking which color you are holding on to if possible. Pay attention to how it affects your energy. The more objectivity, the better. You simply want to determine which color feels the best to you, and which feels the worst. It does not matter how. Worst does not mean it feels bad or negative either; it may be a feeling of dullness, impartiality, or friction.

Go through a process of elimination to narrow them down by separating them into two sets of "maybe best" and "maybe worst" then repeat the process of holding on to them so you are comparing fewer in each pile. Eventually you arrive at "feels best today" and "feels worst today."

Once you have decided on your two, flip back to the Appendix (page 144) to discover your results.

TELEPATHY TASTE TEST

If you enjoyed the first partnering experiment, try a sweet new version now. The two of you are about to put your ultra-sensory taste buds to the test.

In case you have read ahead and landed here, it is recommended for you to do the shared activities in sequence to develop your senses and ability to tune in to each other. The options grow incrementally more challenging. Start with Whatcha Up To? on page 47 before you try the taste test, and I Heard You the First Time following that.

This activity can be done in thirty minutes or an hour, but it may take a day or two to plan, contingent on what supplies you have on hand. Both participants need five different food or candy options. For foods, both you and your accomplice would need one item from each of the five food categories of sweet, salty, bitter, sour, and savory.

If you opt for the candy trail, you will have a hard time keeping away from sweet obviously, so select a range of flavors. Contrasting tastes are perfect, like milk chocolate and dark chocolate, red and black licorice, cinnamon and lemon hard candies, peppermint, caramel, or peanut butter. It is fine if you each have different choices. Try to avoid foods that would be hard to discern between though within your set of five.

If helpful, have some plain crackers and water on hand as palate cleansers between rounds.

For this exercise, take turns back and forth in each round. Do the activity over the phone, or during a video chat, as long as you do not see what the sender is eating. Being on screen also calls for your best poker face to not give away the answer by making a sour lemon drop face.

Decide each of your starting roles, sender and receiver, for the first round. The sender should pop one small piece of an individual food or candy in their mouth and the receiver tries to decide which of the options it is. Close your eyes to concentrate. It is one less sense interfering with your *clairgustance*.

Aside from experiencing a taste in your mouth, there is a likelihood of also smelling the food, since those senses work in unison. If this is the case for you, it is your extended sense of smell, *clairolience*, that would allow for that to happen.

After guessing, the sender can reveal the answer before you switch turns for the round. Go through each round of the foods or try a game of eight or ten rounds where you can repeat food choices, so it is trickier than narrowing it down.

Depending how difficult you want to make this, you can pre-determine "food" or "candy" and not tell each other in advance what the options are. Though that is expert-level challenge. One caveat; how well do you trust your friend? Are they going to get their hands on some fine Wasabi delicacies or the infamous earwax flavored jellybeans for the sake of seeing you cringe when they chomp down? Cringe, or cry.

Keeping your friend once the game is ended is vital. You might want to make a pact.

Oh yes, I have played this game before with students. The idea likely stemmed from my high school days of playing Kitchen Taste Test with my neighbor, a real comedian. Non-chewable Vitamin C tablet. I still recollect that round.

Clairgustance: The ability to taste by ultra-sensory means; "clear-tasting." From French, clair *(clear) + Latin* gustare *(to taste).*

Clairolience: The ability to smell by ultra-sensory means; "clear-smelling." From French, clair *(clear) + Latin* olere *(to smell of; to smell like).*

I HEARD YOU the FIRST TIME

This is another partnering activity. Try Whatcha Up To? *and* Telepathy Taste Test *before moving on to this third exercise.*

Take on another shared challenge with version three of the collaborative experiments, a telepathic listening game.

Once again, determine the timeframe for your test and set that plan in place, like you did with the first Whatcha Up To? game. If you tried it a couple different ways, use what worked well before, whether over the course of a day, three days, or a week. It is up to you again, the effort you invest in the practice. The importance is that you are on the same page with the sending and receiving schedule.

In this game, choose two phrases or simple messages to send each other, selecting at random and sending one per scheduled time. You cannot think about which one to send when the timer goes off because trying to decide sends both, so choose which message in advance is to be delivered on time. If possible, add it as your timer note. It is a reliable way to keep a record of what you sent, which is critical to validate the receiver's experiences at the end. Once again, set and synchronize your timers. You have less than a minute to tune in to the other person, so accuracy is needed.

If you are distractible you may want to include plain gestures, like putting a hand on your heart paired with one message and folding your hands together for the second, as an example. Having a physical gesture may support the sender to not mix up the two thoughts.

Decide which messages to send. These should be as different as possible, so they do not sound the same. Examples to work with include:

> I am so grateful for you.
> You make me laugh.
> Remember when we went to _____?
> _____ is my favorite color.
> Someday we should go to _____ together.
> You are so good at _____.
> I appreciate you for _____.
> Do you know that I like _____?
> Have a happy day.
> You've got this.
> I think you are _____.

As the sender, when the timer goes off, think through the one message, repeating it several times.

This is optional, but for some who are new to the idea of telepathy, or those who already know that clairvoyance is their strongest ultra-sense, instead of having a gesture paired to the message, you could try pairing each message with a basic image. This would be the sender communicating, "Have a happy day," while at the same time imagining a red balloon. It could also be sending the words "you have got this" along with the image of a golden trophy. Discuss your preferences, as you can always redo the experiment with different dynamics.

The receiver should record what they think they picked up on telepathically. For different people or situations, the way the information is perceived may be via the sense of knowing (*claircognizance*), but even more so by hearing the thought (*clairaudience*). Of course, compare notes at the end of the entire experiment, not during. Reserve judgment and be supportive of each other through the trials and errors. Mistakes may happen for several reasons. The biggest obstacle is always self-doubt, but you have the choice to keep one another above that and to thoughtfully find explanations, rather than excuses. These activities are all about discovering your natural, individual abilities. It should not be anticipated that people process sensory information the same exact way. The opportunity is in being able to distinguish your personal strengths and by that, improve confidence in your inner voice.

In reviewing the outcomes together, do make note of which times of day or which messages resulted in superior accuracy. Work around that when you revisit the game.

Want a bigger challenge? Plan for additional rounds to practice. Build up the number of phrases for the sender to choose between and extend the length of play, adding on days or weeks.

Clairaudience: The ability to distinguish sound by ultra-sensory means; the faculty of hearing something not perceptible to the ear; "clear hearing." From French, clair *(clear)* + *Latin,* audire *(to hear).*

Telepathy: Non-verbal communication between a sender and receiver; communicating by using ultra-sensory means to transfer emotional, mental, or physical messages.

CATCHY

One other way to Get Soundtracked (page 56) is by using a CD or record collection. This can be a slightly different experience because it involves the sense of touch and the ultra-sensory extension of that, *clairsentience*.

For this activity, think of one question and record that on the top of your paper. It is important to do that so there is no confusion over what you landed on asking. If you have other questions in mind, you can write those too, leaving room in between each. No more than five is reasonable, at least until you see how the exercise works for you.

With your first question in mind, and your CDs or vinyls in front of you, ask of the Universe, your higher self, or spirit guides, "Which number?" Count in order (left to right, top to bottom, or front to back), based on how you have your collection stored, to select out that number album. Alternately, think, "Tell me when to stop," and run

AWARENESS ACTIVITIES

your finger across the spines of the cases slowly until you land on the right one. Depending on your capabilities, it is a feeling or thought. Some feel like their hand stops moving, while others have the thought "stop" come to mind. There is no one exact approach.

When you have the album in hand, your next step is to get the correct track. Run a finger over the contents list or ask your higher self for which number track to play. Then set it up to listen. If you can, follow along with a lyrics sheet. Again, the message may be the title of the song, or it could be found within the verses. Either way, it tends to supplement a sense of knowing (*claircognizance*).

And there you have your message. Repeat the process for all the questions in your list. By the end you have lots to ponder, and maybe a tiny earworm to make sure the important parts catch. The waiting and hoping for any sort of connection is over, with prospects for developing this channel of communication.

Claircognizance: The ultra-sense of knowing; the sixth sense; "clear-knowing." From French, clair *(clear) + Latin,* cognoscere *(to know).*

The first time I was made aware of this kind of activity it was completely unexpected. I later adapted my personal experience to this version for my students. Anyway, that initial time a young client and I were chatting online. Her husband, who had passed away, was relaying messages to her through me. He asked me to go over to my CD tower and told me to choose a certain disc, then had me play it while we were talking. When we got to a precise track he interjected into the conversation, "This is the song for her," so I shared that sweet musical message. Of course, the artist, the song lyrics and title, all had an immediate impact for her.

That is the thing about messages. Whether it is our own higher self, our spirit guides, or our passed loved ones, if they hope for us to grasp an important idea, they keep trying to get the words across. The primary gift in that is knowing that they are okay, they are with us, and that we are not going through life alone.

SIGN of the TIMES

Along with all these activities, we cannot forget the basic idea of asking for a sign. Someone in the Universe has a message for you. Here is how to get it.

Choose one of the animals from the list that follows. There does not have to be any reasoning behind it. Try not to second guess yourself. Ask by thinking, "Please deliver the divinely timed message to me by sending a sign of a _____ (your chosen animal)."

After you ask, put it out of your mind. Actively looking for the animal, holding it in the front of your thoughts, would mean any occurrence of the animal would not count. A sign always catches you by surprise. They show up when we are concentrating on other matters, in unanticipated ways, in unusual forms. You could anticipate receiving a rabbit sign and end up having a waitress named Bunny, for example. This is why you ask and let it go. Your higher self or guides will be excited to show you in a precise way and time.

ANIMAL OPTIONS

Chimpanzee
Dolphin
Lion
Penguin
Rabbit
Wolf

As I went back to title this exercise, I realized I did not know what I should call it. My guides told me to use a search engine and the title would be the first suggestion that came up as I began typing. S-i-g...Sign of the Times. How fitting considering all that is going on in the world. It is not always that easy to be certain about messages though. It takes practice and often, extra communication.

Once you have your sign crop up, if you are unclear about it, ask for confirmation and wait for a repeated sign in a distinct way. If you feel like you were looking for it around every corner, you probably were. Receiving a true sign makes you do a double take or feel amazement. When you are sure you got your sign, look up your animal to receive your corresponding message in the No Peeking Section (page 152).

PART TWO
Tarot Games

Dust off that tarot deck and shuffle up some insight. The various games are resources to get to know your deck better and to build confidence around that. It is not meant for learning how to use tarot in a traditional or strict way. Challenge your spiritual and sensory acuity while enjoying the process. Part of experimenting this way means that when and if needed for supporting your interpretations, it is okay to reference the guidebook that comes with your deck or a trustworthy book, like *Tarot Plain and Simple*, by Anthony Louis or *The Ultimate Guide to Tarot* by Liz Dean.

There is no reason someone entirely new to *cartomancy* (divination by use of a card deck) or tarot more exactly, cannot have the same success with the activities as someone who knows their cards inside and out. For those in the latter group, there are always intricacies to learn and new perspectives to be discovered.

In going through the tarot games, if you are confused by any results, set them aside and ask the Universe for further explanation. If it makes no sense to you whatsoever, try it again another day. Our moods, mindset, and energy affect all parts of life, that includes how well the exercises work. Serious, sarcastic, sappy, silly, or saucy; what you bring into it comes back out with you.

A CROSS TICK

Here is how to conquer that one card that makes you draw a blank when you look at it.

A simple acquainting activity, this is purely for entertainment, but it is also a chance to learn more about your deck. You need your tarot cards, paper, and pen. While possible to repeat this activity 78 times to inspect the whole lot of cards, and to repeat again...to infinity, we will shoot a tad lower for now. Choose one card. Especially if you are new to tarot or if you are working with a deck that is brand new to you, opt for a major arcana card over a minor (suit) card.

If you do not have one that immediately comes to mind, separate your major cards out and briefly look through them to find a card that is harder for you to define. Maybe it is difficult to put into words, or it is unfamiliar, or you find it confusing. An ideal card to choose for this exercise is one that always stumps you. That card has a place, and this is its starring moment.

Perhaps you recall from school days doing an *acrostic* as a poetry assignment, or maybe you once handcrafted a Mother's Day card in such fashion. The acrostic tarot game goes like this. Using the title of the selected card, write each letter of the card name on one line going down the left side of your paper. Then, to the right of the letters, write an adjective or short phrase about the card's general meaning. Always begin with the first letter.

Following are two partial examples, using the Moon card. Complete them if you like or get started with your own. For retention of the contrast, it is a good idea to do one acrostic for the upright card and one for the reversal of it. Unless you chose the Knight of Pentacles, with the longest title, it is a speedy game.

Single Words:

M	ystery
O	ceanic
O	
N	

Phrases:

M	ysterious night
O	verwhelming depth of emotion
O	
N	

Once completed, this becomes a little memory to tap into while using your deck in times to come. When the card eventually resurfaces, the keywords you use to create your acrostic will enrich meaning for you. It is plenty to build definitive explanations on in a tarot spread.

As a side note, the title of this activity is in reference to The Hanged Man card in the *Arthropoda Tarot Deck* by Norwegian artist, Linda Ursin. It goes to show there are decks with artwork to suit every interest and personality.

SEVEN ELEVENS TAROT

With this convenient end-of-the-day activity, the goal is to draw one card from your deck meant for a highlight about the following day. Rather than focusing on basic or traditional card meanings, like one would for a typical message-of-the-day tarot reading, we will simplify this.

In your journal, plan by recording the days of the week, starting with whatever day tomorrow is. Leave room for your comments between each day. Beginning in the middle or end of a calendar week is fine. If you are finding it worthwhile doing this every day for a week, of course you can extend past that in weekly increments.

Shuffle your deck as you would normally. Cut the deck in two. With your deck restacked and face down, count from the top and take out the eleventh card.

The first detail you notice in the card is your symbol for the following day. Do not worry about what the card is or the meaning behind it. In this exercise you are familiarizing yourself with traits of the cards and the artwork. Write about whatever it is you saw and include a short, simple interpretation about what it means to you. What does it make you think of or feel like? Perhaps it reminds you of another object or of an experience. Whatever it is, try not to question it and take it as a sort of clue for the day.

On the following day, as you wind down at night, reflect on how that symbol or clue played a part or was clarified. Then, repeat the process the exact same way for tomorrow. At the end of the week you will have drawn out seven elevens.

A note about the first attribute you see. When you flip the card, what you glimpse may not be a central object, which is excellent. It could be a trait, color, word, design, feeling it evokes, or action it portrays. Maybe at first glance you are drawn to an element in the picture, then looking at it further, see it is a completely different object.

As an example in that instance, your entry for the night might read, "My card for Wednesday is the 8 of Swords. What I noticed first was a leaf on the ground, which turned out to be a lizard upon closer inspection." You would follow, of course, by writing what the leaf symbolizes to you, as well as the lizard if you felt importance in the duality. Or, perhaps you were only meant to see it as a leaf. There is not a singular correct way to critique it, other than what suits you. It is about the mindfulness cultivated by listening to your inner voice.

ESCAPE into a CARD

Exploring scenery and backgrounds in your deck is the priority with this contemplation and journaling task. Escape into one of the two variations that follow.

ONE

The simplest approach to this is sorting through your deck to find a card that has a background you find appealing in the moment.

Imagine this scenery came to life and you could visit. Spend some time musing on this. Journal what it would be like to get away to that place. Is it realistic or other-worldly? Include aspects perceived by all of your senses in the description you write.

TWO

Put your deck scenery and background to work for you. Either separate out every card in the deck that has a picturesque background you can work with or go wild and take a chance using the entire deck.

While you are shuffling, think to yourself or say out loud, "Show me where my next dream vacation ought to be." If a single card flies out of your deck, that is your card, otherwise shuffle until you feel you should stop, cut your deck as usual, and count downwards from the top, five cards: D-R-E-A-M. That fifth one is yours for the journaling and reflection. As with the first version, imagine this is a representation of an actual place you can travel to one day. Let it come to life in your thoughts. Where is the location? What attributes in the card may be hints as to the place or perhaps to a few symbolic messages about your dream vacation? Is there a clue about travel companions?

For either version, feel free to take this one step further and go into a full meditation about your scene, using that as the backdrop to explore or ask questions. Do elements appear that are not depicted in the card itself? Is anything distinctly different from the artwork? Unexpected finds may carry clues. With the second version, create an affirmation to manifest this magnificent dream into being.

TAROT SPY

A completely different way to use your tarot deck for the symbols in the artwork is through this *I Spy* game. You do not need a question in advance to play either, so the worst part is already out of the way. (Now and then everyone flounders to think of questions to ask when practicing tarot). Have paper and pen ready to record your answers, listed 1 through 5, and then to journal about the findings.

Shuffle up your deck as usual. If you prefer to cut it into piles and restack it, do that, too.

Fan out the cards like a poker boss, face down.

Select nine cards to form into a rectangle, placing them face up in order as shown in the diagram. Keep them upright or reversed as they appear.

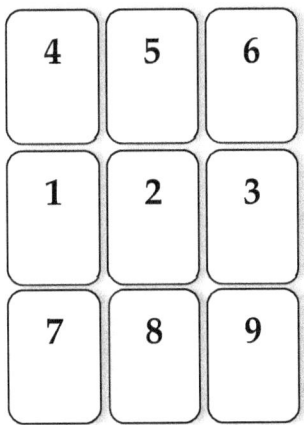

Work through the following list in order, recording your answers completely before sneaking a peek of the Appendix. Write the first answer that draws attention in each instance. Do not scan through to pick a card you prefer. A card may be used as an answer more than once. At least three of the cards will not be used.

FIND...	Found in this CARD
A circle	
Something that looks shiny	
What is or looks like a vine, cord, ribbon, string, or rope	
Something showing wind, or action/motion/movement	
Something edible	
Something green	

Continued in the No Peeking Section, page 174.

TIMES are a-CHANGIN'

One topic always surfaces when it comes to self-awareness. That is the idea of purpose. People who are awakening and invested in their spiritual nature are compelled to deliberate action when it comes to jobs, hobbies, and how time is spent. It is less about keeping up with that Jones family and ego-based priorities, and more about wanting to be on the right track, feeling pulled to serve their highest good. Spiritually evolved people have an intrinsic need to fulfill whatever their soul had planned for them when they set out on another human adventure.

Here we pair tarot with a whisper of self-reflection on the topic of purpose, to ease a perplexing time. Whether it is an internal coaxing to make a change or a forced transitional time, putting a few thoughts on paper contributes toward making decisions. An oracle deck may work for this exercise as well.

Shuffle your deck and as you do, think to yourself, "Please show me how I am changing and where this transition is leading me."

When you stop shuffling, cut the deck into three piles, and restack the deck however you choose. Starting with the top card, place your cards in the numbered succession shown, face down.

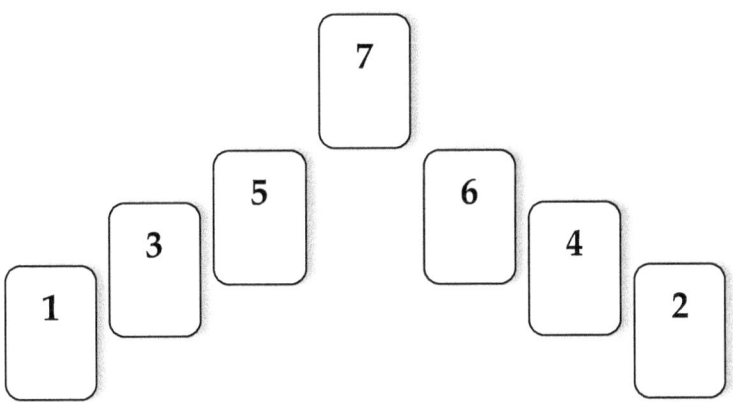

Once you have the spread laid out, turn over and study one card at a time, going in the same order. First, record the initial three observations about the card. Objects, qualities, characters, feeling, motion/movement, a word, a symbol. There are not wrong answers and there is no need to second guess yourself. Pay attention to what is eye-catching, without analyzing it.

Second, write a little bit about what you noted, any thoughts you have about them. That may include symbolism, personal experience, or an explanation of what it makes you feel or think about when you flipped the card.

Third, write up to three general words or phrases based on the traditional meanings of the card. Use your deck guidebook if you are new to the cards. Only write what is first notable. It is never about *all* the words.

After you have finished this process with all seven cards, then go to the No Peeking Section, page 190, for information about the cards' designated purposes. With that then you can do a full interpretation.

NOTE on CHANGE

Apart from this, for anyone facing an adversity there are considerations. To not breeze by someone who may be feeling stuck or distressed with a flip of a few tarot cards, here is an idea about change to contemplate from a spiritual perspective. The *bigger picture* if you will. Apply the thoughts in order to navigate your own circumstance should you wish.

What looks or feels like ruin, is not meant to *be* ruin. It is meant to move you on to some other course in life. It is designed for *good* and for serving a soul-driven purpose.

That may be about awareness or understanding that induces an evolution in character. It may be about inciting a shift in careers, relationships, lifestyle, or residence. That is only to mention a few possibilities, because they are countless.

You are meant to experience the human emotions of the event, yes. That is part of being here, to understand the human experience. Beyond that though, discern how the pain or ruinous feeling is about looking back, being tethered to how it was. If you see how it is affecting your situation, then you can make a shift. When you are prepared to, of course, because all that matters is you honoring your process. But at that time, ask for the good to be exposed. From there start to refocus to see what beauty, possibility, and blessings are trying to make their way in. Once you ask, the transformation and the energy involved with it take on an utterly different creative frequency. This shift allows for the good, better, *and* best to enter your life.

Assume your soul knows the way. It absolutely has your life plan at heart. Hold on to that faith and let it guide you.

Now, back to our regularly planned shenanigans.

YOU DO YOU HAIKU

For this little pastime, choose three cards from your tarot deck by any means that strike your fancy and set them face up in a sequence that looks acceptable to you. It does not have to be in the order you selected them.

Now you can call upon Matsuo Basho or Ezra Pound for inspiration if you must, but the objective is getting to know your cards a bit better. With a little investigating and thought, it should be enough to come up with a quick Tarot Haiku of your own making.

As a refresher, a haiku is a short poem with only three lines. The first and third lines have five syllables and the second line has seven. Punctuation and capitalization are up to you as the poet. It is rare to rhyme the lines, so that makes it easier.

Use each card you drew as a reference for respective lines, or choose one of the three cards as a focus for the whole poem. Write about the picture, distinct aspects, the character, the meaning, or the symbolism. Incorporate keywords so if you were to write ten different poems, you would be able to identify the cards you used as reference.

Typically, haiku are in reverence of nature, so adding elements of seasons and environment depicted by your cards would conform your haiku to tradition.

There are no right or wrong answers. Maybe some terrible haiku, but no one is grading. Hypothetically, it could be a gateway to limericks. In any case, here are three examples, written specially for the occasion.

TAROT GAMES

> ❂ *Emotional string*
> *A devoted person speaks*
> *Betrayed by the pause*

> ❂ *Duality moves*
> *Reining progress past delay*
> *Master of my fate*

> ❂ *Promise between loves*
> *Energy bound by divide*
> *Still, waiting for word*

ADDED OPTION

If you are well-acquainted with tarot already, you may wish to use this as a divination exercise. Ask a question. Shuffle and draw your three cards (or one if you are keeping it simple). Then, write the haiku based on the overall message or story that the three cards tell, as an answer to your question.

This can work to your advantage for a poem truer to haiku, with two opposing or unrelated ideas presented in the first two lines. Use one card per line. Include a traditional haiku "cutting word," dividing the poem into two sections, and you are a master.

Haiku do not need to have titles. Customarily, the first line acts as the title. But if you try haiku for answering a question, it is recommended that you record your question in your journal first. Then, use the drawn cards as the title (in any way you can personally identify them later; they do not need to be spelled out). After that, write your haiku on the following lines. In the end it is a reminder of why you wrote what you did. This is useful in case you revisit the answer. It also is helpful if your inner haikuist wants to create a new responsive poem from hindsight of events.

ONE THING LEADS to ANOTHER

To understand a situation, take a look at how differing angles of it connect. In this tarot practice you want to think of a personal example to use as your focus. You may know where an issue stands now, but what follows? What is the cause or purpose? This exercise attempts to bring clarity.

Your deck should be shuffled as usual while you think about the situation. Split the deck into three piles. Flip over the top card on each pile.

Journal a few notes about these three cards and the sequence displayed, as to how it relates to your situation at hand. Determine which card best represents the present moment. Any cards behind that portray roots of an issue and the past, while cards ahead of it give an outlook for moving forward. It may well hint toward what is yet to come, so with a little advance awareness it prepares you to handle it sensibly.

For instance, if it is the third card that most reflects the present, understand the root of the situation, and keep on track to continue. If it is the first card that you feel represents the situation, you likely understand the past, but needed input about what the steps ahead may entail. Consider what is being shown so you can make informed decisions, be prepared, or proceed in a way that is in your best interest.

CALL a DO OVER

Think of a least favorite card you want to use for this activity. Or, shuffle through your deck until you find one you do not like as much, by design or because you find it hard to explain. The reasoning is not imperative. Finding new acceptance for this card is the goal.

Write the name of the card as your header in your journal. Spend a moment looking over the artwork, both upright and reversed.

Below the title, write what it is that you do not care for about the card. A sentence or two is plenty.

Following that, make a list of six positive keywords and six negative keywords the card represents. Try to come up with these on your own before resorting to a guidebook. Consequentially, you arrive at the root of what the card represents to you, in your words. This might illustrate why you dislike it.

Now, imagine that this card came up for you in a reading in the past. Write a little about why it might have surfaced. What events were taking place in your life that relate to the card? Is the dislike for the card about the card itself or is about a reminder of an unpleasantry in your past that perhaps is not healed? If this is the case, then there are steps you can take to change that and be able to divide out that the card is just a card. Ultimately you do not need it to appear as an unending reminder of this history, consciously or subconsciously. All that would do is negatively sway future spreads in which it turns up.

Add on to the end a concise phrase or sentence that summons up the meaning of the card for you. This does not mean that it applies in every instance of readings, but rather is a launching point to get your thoughts on track toward its unique meaning in a spread. For example, seeing the Star card may make you think, "A wish is coming true," or, the Hanged Man sparks the initial thought, "a different perspective," as a reminder that looking at the situation in question from a new angle is imperative.

Card Title:

Keywords, positive:

Keywords, negative:

Summary Phrase:

Lastly, look over what you have written and the card imagery again. Is there a part you feel is missing from it, whether in the title, meaning, keywords, or symbolism within the artwork?

With the writing portion of the exercise done, make a little sketch to redesign the card in a way that makes you have an appreciation for it, or at least a neutrality. It does not need to be pretty. Include the aspects from the original version, plus additions or changes that make you satisfied with the card.

From this point on, any time the original card comes up you will carry this meaningful version in your mind to guide you over any hurdles with the interpretation.

WHAT I TRULY WANT

Use this activity to get to the heart of a matter. On day one, decide what issue you want to address. That will not be difficult. It sticks in your mind. This is an issue about a lacking component. It is a part of life you want to resolve, change, or grow.

First, get clear on the matter. Write in your journal for a few minutes about what you have been thinking about the situation up until this moment. Do not forget to end with the part about what you are either doing about it now or planning on (you know, the *expectations* slice of pie.)

Second, when you are done summarizing, set the intention that one single card will fall out as you shuffle your deck. As you do, think to yourself, "What do I *truly* want?" Check out the card that shakes loose. Write some notes. Take it in. Give yourself the night to sleep on it.

The following day, (or two, if it is needed to wrap your mind around it all) repeat the shuffling. This time ask about acceptance and how to allow what you truly want to manifest in your life. Again, take the single card that springs out of the deck as you shuffle.

From there, add some interpretive notes about this in your journal. You may wish to use an affirmation to solidify this, such as, "I truly want _____. Let it be so." Simple enough. Trust your soul and the higher-ups to handle it. Take action as opportunities arise. If you need more than that, spend some time in meditation on the matter to find out specifics or ask questions.

TAROT ZOO

Thirty to sixty minutes may be needed for this activity from start to finish, so you can plan for that.

PART ONE

Have you ever noticed how many animals are hiding in your tarot cards? While some cards, such as Strength, have an obvious one like the lion, others have subtle or hidden characters. They are all put there for a reason and for symbolism the artists find important.

TAROT ZOO MAP

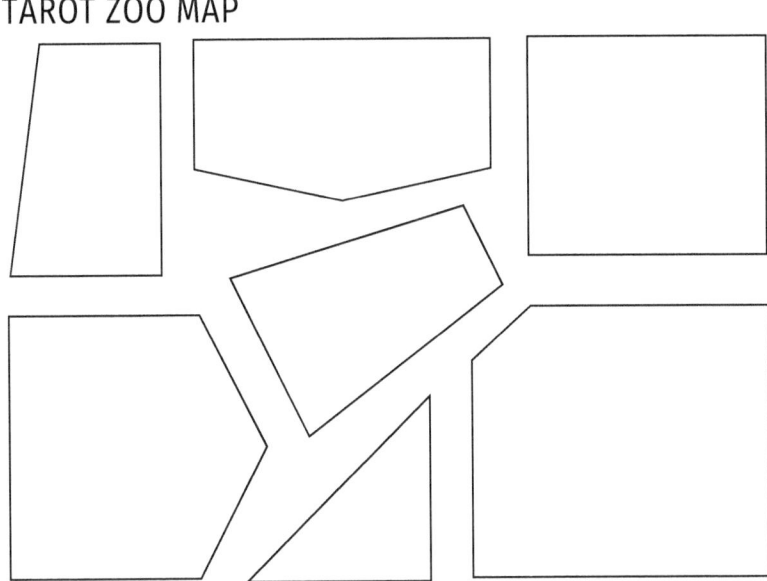

For this game, go through your traditional tarot deck to locate animals.

1. Shuffle and cut your deck as usual.
2. Work from the top card downwards looking for animals to put in your zoo.
3. When you come across an animal, put them in enclosures as pictured below. You may write names in the boxes if you wish but keep track of the cards setting each animal card into one of seven piles to reflect which enclosure area they are in, according to the diagram. You will need the cards later.
4. If you have a card depicting multiple animals, choose only one of them and include that animal/card with the enclosure you select.

5. Put up to four per enclosure only. There are no regulations about how you combine them, so do not dwell on logic. (They are not real; there is no worry about them chewing on each other.)
6. You can fill the enclosures or leave some empty as you wish. That is entirely up to you.

When satisfied with your zoo, look at the Tarot Zoo Map and select *one* of the enclosures. Keep the piles of cards where they are but flip them all face down, except for the stack that corresponds to the enclosure you chose. Put those cards in a row so you can see them. After that, go to the No Peeking Section (page 180) for the next two tasks.

ON a BRIGHTER DAY

This too shall pass. We all know that saying. Now, to amplify the hopeful meaning of the mantra. Here we can turn our focus toward better days yet to come.

The initial step is to ask for a sign. In this instance, we ask and set the intention for a first name. Like so. "Please send me a repeating sign that is the name of a person, soon coming into my life for a positive reason." Do not define the reason, your higher self knows what it is. Humor, mentoring, friendship, love, or authentically being of help to you in a needed way. Keep from setting expectation so it leaves all the possibilities wide open. Though, do not assume every person with that name is the right person.

You will know absolutely the one they mean for you to meet. Trust the divine timing.

Let it go once you ask. But over the coming days or weeks, take note of a name that is repeating itself in different ways. The sign will imaginably have varying sources and happen in several places. This could come by reading the name in a book, seeing it on a sign or name tag, hearing it over an intercom speaker, radio, or television. Someone may even say the name while you are standing in line waiting to check out. However it comes, make a mental note of it. The minimum of occurrences should be three, but if you are dubious or you miss one here and there, it will come back around another way. As usual, it does not count if you are actively looking, waiting for it to happen.

After you put the request out to the Universe, shuffle your deck as you ask for a clue regarding the person. Stop when you feel you should and cut the deck. Take only the top card and see what you spot about it quickly. Make a note of what you think your clue or sign is in your journal, so you have that to refer to if needed. If you cannot decide between two attributes, add both. One will become prominent. The clue may turn up to alert you to the name signs coming your way, or it may end up being a hint for you when the person arrives. This all depends on your circumstance and connection with higher self, so again, do not hold expectation over it. Let the Universe handle the magic. And now, there is a nice little light at the end of the tunnel for you to look toward with hope and excitement as you navigate through a challenging time.

ANOTHER OPTION

If you wish to glean signs about a place or an opportunity, instead of a person, those are valid alternatives. Do the asking for one of those instead. Again, do not anticipate the place or opportunity, or what its positive association will be for you; let it be presented. That way it comes together effectively, with no interference. Let your subconscious alert you to repetition of the place, by names or pictures.

In either instance, keep notes of happenings in your journal as it is amazing to see synchronicities lining up.

TAROT SPY SOLITAIRE

Shuffle your deck as you like.

Starting from the top card, flip one at a time. Look for one card to fit the qualification for each of the five spaces as seen in the diagram. You do not have to go in order one through five, but do place the cards in the correct spaces. Choose the first card that comes up that applies in an instance. Do not sift through all the cards to find other options. If a card does not fit into one of the five spaces, place it face down in a discard pile.

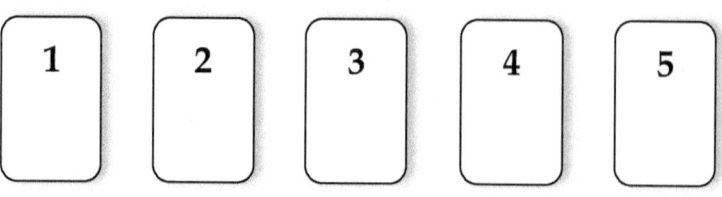

Card 1: Something that looks like a door (a rectangle).
Card 2: Something not a part of your daily life.
Card 3: An article of clothing.
Card 4: Something edible.
Card 5: A hidden object is in the picture.

With the remaining cards, if you have less than 25 in hand, cut the discard pile in two and add *one* of those halves to the bottom of your deck. If you have more than 25, then only use the deck as it is for the remainder of the activity.

Working from the top card downwards, flip one at a time. Make an association with any aspect found in one of the five starting cards. Such as, the flipped card has a tree in it and that matches the tree in the fourth column. It does not need to be based on the starter row qualifications and it can be a match for any reason, with one exception. Do not place a suit card on top of another matching suit card, unless all five face up cards are matching that suit. In other words, you cannot count coins, swords, wands, or cups as a reason to match. Instead, look for other objects, colors, shapes, animals, and qualities to make the match. Only make matches with the topmost card in each column, not with those beneath it.

Go through every card in your hand to make five columns of cards. It does not matter the quantity of cards in a column; it is expected they will be uneven. Once you have placed them all, move on to the No Peeking Section (page 179) to find the next steps.

AWKWARD FAMILY TAROT

It is normal that cards come up in a tarot reading to represent people in our lives, only not all at once. During this easy, card-familiarization game you will apply all the court card personalities to your friends, family, and acquaintances. Whoever is in your circle, or circle-adjacent, is fair game. Play at your own risk and try to not pit the Montagues against the Capulets.

To start, take all the minor arcana court cards out of your deck and separate them into suits. If you like you can lay them all out face up. Though it is not necessary, if you do not want all those eyes on you as you decide their fates.

For the game, attempt to go by traditional intention of cards and suits to become more accustomed to the characters and personality traits. Adjust the court titles in the chart to match your cards if need be. Pages and knights may be princes and princesses, or a king may be called guardian. In the event you have a deck with unusual court cards, make sure to study the guidebook and see what qualities are assigned by the author as they may swerve away from tradition. It will be worthwhile for you to know the simliarities and differences as you continue to use your deck. If you have a reason to change an aspect in the list to match your own deck, that is fine, they are your cards after all.

Essentially the activity goes like this, a description is given for each suit and court card. Look over your own cards as references as you assign a person you know to each. How you place them is up to you. It is a fluid game without an answer key, but there should still be reasoning behind your choices. Include details about that in your notes if you like. Remember to include yourself in the assigning. It is only fair. Afterall, you are a most likely candidate to emerge in tarot readings for yourself.

Regarding age factors, pages are typically children or young people. Knights denote teens or young adults. In some circumstances they represent a peer connected to the person asking the questions for a tarot reading. Such an instance is when it represents a person's knight in shining armor, regardless of their ages. The queen and king are generally mature adults. They may signify peer-age people to an adult querent, such as a partner. Sometimes they stand for elders or people of authority.

A couple other notes on portrayals. While it is true that the majority of tarot decks lack representation of cultural diversity, there are some newer decks filling that void. Decks by Kris Waldherr and Kim Huggens are a good place to start your search for elaborate, multicultural cards, suited for all levels of ability. The downside with a few recent decks is that the creators have taken other drastic liberties. Even though they are lovely decks, that makes them difficult for those new to tarot to use. The recommendation here is to begin with a conventional deck to build foundation and understanding, then branch out from there. Do know that whether or not the character portrayed is a look-a-like, the suits have always been intended to represent people with differing complexions and appearances. Those specifications are included in the suit listings of this activity for reference.

This applies to gender as well. Practical advice is to consider the character and fluid energy (masculine or feminine) of the person as factors rather than following strictly male or female roles. As examples, a king card turns up to represent a masculine-energy female or to emphasize a woman who is an authoritative figure running her own company. How does one figure all those intricacies out? That is where development of ultra-sensory abilities comes in; give it time. And, practice.

Beyond that, cards reflect situations; people's behaviors are changeable. Because of this, one card is never a constant, absolute depiction for a person. It is necessary to evaluate every instance. When court cards or characters of the major arcana turn up in a spread, the question that was asked and the conditions behind it are the context for deciding who the characters signify. The representation is then based on personality, situational behaviors, and inner selves, not strictly outer appearances.

With Awkward Family Tarot, instead of going solely on logic, give your ultra-senses a workout if you are up for it. For each character, think to yourself, "Who does this card represent right now?" See what name or face comes to you.

If you cannot think of anyone you know who fits one of the spaces, try to think of a fictional character who exemplifies the role instead. If it happens to be one of the villainous ones, find some wood to gratefully knock that you are not dealing with a person like that in your life.

PENTACLES

Characters in the pentacles or coins suit often have brown or black hair, dark eyes, and darker skin tone.

UPRIGHT

Page	Student, bookworm, honest	
Knight	Dependable, hard-working	
Queen	Kind, generous, leader	
King	Stable, ambitious, provider	

REVERSED

Page	Irresponsible, moody, defiant	
Knight	Dim, uninspired, lazy	
Queen	Self-important, busybody	
King	Mean, greedy, materialistic	

SWORDS

Characters in the swords or epees suit often have brown or black hair, light eyes, and medium or olive skin tone.

UPRIGHT

Page	Bright, curious, witty child	
Knight	Gallant, intellectual	
Queen	Courageous, survivor, teacher	
King	Intimidating, authoritative	

REVERSED

Page	Juvenile delinquent, conniver	
Knight	Bossy, troublemaker	
Queen	Vindictive, bitter, shrew	
King	Ruthless, cold-hearted bully	

CUPS

Characters in the cups or chalices suit often have blonde, light brown, or gray hair, blue, hazel, or light eyes, and medium or fair skin tone.

UPRIGHT

Page	Friendly, creative, intuitive	
Knight	Romantic, attentive dreamer	
Queen	Perceptive, devoted, caring	
King	Educated, stable, trustworthy	

REVERSED

Page	Selfish, slack, attention seeker	
Knight	Deceptive, narcissist	
Queen	Superficial, vapid, fickle	
King	Sleazy, manipulative, creeper	

WANDS

Characters in the wands or staves suit often have blonde, red, or light-colored hair, dark or light eyes, and fair or freckled skin tone.

UPRIGHT

Page	Charming chatterbox, helpful	
Knight	Fun-loving, adventurous	
Queen	Amiable, talented, organizer	
King	Optimistic, generous, adventurer	

REVERSED

Page	Sneaky one, entitled, devious	
Knight	Argumentative, opportunist	
Queen	Petty, gold-digger, unreliable	
King	Arrogant, intolerant, con man	

A STEP FURTHER

If you want an extra assignment for entertainment, take the "suit families" you have originated, or select one or two of the archetypes that amuse you, and write a short story or song about your characters. Creativity can be ignited in unexpected places. No added rules or input, except these five words: pseudonyms, work of fiction disclaimer.

REVERSE TAROT

In the moment you want to try this activity, stop what you are doing and take a landscape picture with your phone or digital camera. If inside, try to shoot a photograph out your window. No thinking about it, no framing, no one focal point or setting up a scene. An unplanned snapshot of a moment in time, quite as it is. If it needs to be an indoor shot, that does the job, but capture a whole scene, not a closeup.

Once you have the photo, you can collect your journal and pen for the next part.

Reverse Tarot is all about making up your own tarot card on the fly. Looking at your photo, imagine this is a new tarot card. Use the chart on the next page as a guideline to fill in for your journal. Begin with identifying up to ten items in the picture. Assign a symbolic meaning to each. These will be your card keywords.

Next, give your card a title. Decide if it is a major or minor arcana card. If a minor card, which suit would you assign it to? Wands for spirit, work and career. Cups for emotions and love. Swords for knowledge, thoughts, and ideas. Pentacles for power, finances and means. Include a number to indicate where you want it to fit in between other cards, like, "4.5 of Pentacles."

If you are not entirely accustomed to your deck yet, choose a suit, then use your guidebook to reference cards of that suit. Determine the placement with that guidance.

As a final step of Reverse Tarot, if you wish, imagine you drew this newly created card as a message-of-the-day for tomorrow. Interpret that with a sentence or two, concluding your notes.

ITEMS	SYMBOLISM/KEYWORDS

Major or Minor Arcana:	
Name of Card:	
Number of Card:	

Message-of-the-Day:

LUNE-a-DAY

Try your hand at penning another poem. With three lines like the haiku, the lune, also called *American haiku*, is even shorter. It is a thirteen-syllable poem that has five syllables in the first and third lines and only three syllables in the middle line. No other rules apply. Not of rhyming, punctuation, or capitalization, nor of themes or cutting words. If it looks like a crescent moon (*lune*) in the end, you have written a picture-perfect lune.

The poem you create can be used as your own poetic message-of-the-day. Shuffle your deck and select a single card. Try to use the first aspect of the card that you perceive as one of the words in your lune. As you compose your poem, ponder what circumstance may be the reason for this particular card to come up. That awareness brings more meaning to the exercise.

A couple tarot lune samples are given, but for expert lunes one should reference the creator, Robert Kelly.

> *Good news arriving*
> *Patience wins*
> *Serendipitous*

> *Tangible progress*
> *Offer made*
> *Come toward at last*

MORE LUNES

Do not run out of free-time pursuits. Try this variation of lune poems, too.

The *Collum lune* is structured with three *words* in the first line, five words in the middle line, and again three words in the last line, regardless of syllable count. Tarot samples are included. Can you guess which cards were the themes for all the lunes?

> ❦ *Twist of fate*
> *Opening the door up wide*
> *Finally, a chance*

> ❦ *Wield big talent*
> *Creative forces on display; to*
> *accept first blessing*

BESIDE MYSELF

Put your tarot cards to work for you when you are feeling beside yourself, stuck, or unable to focus. This quick activity sorts your priorities or brings a distraction to get you back on course.

While oracle decks not based on a tarot format cannot be used for this, you could use a standard deck of playing cards. It also works with a tarot deck that has plain minor arcana cards.

Give your cards a speedy mix and in your own words, ask for guidance to prioritize what is vital to focus on in the moment. Cut the deck if you wish, based on your usual routine.

When you stop, hold the deck in one hand, cards face down. With the other, turn one card at a time, placing it in the appropriate pile as directed. Major arcana cards that do not apply may be set aside in a separate discard pile.

Pile 1: A PERSON – from any suit, or arcana.
Pile 2: Wands/Rods/Staves or Clubs.
Pile 3: Cups/Chalices or Hearts.
Pile 4: Swords/Epees or Spades.
Pile 5: Pentacles/Coins or Diamonds.

Flip through your cards, dividing them into piles until one has five cards stacked in it. This pile is your answer. Check page 142 of the No Peeking Section to get to the corresponding guidance.

TAROT SPY MISSION

Your mission, should you choose to accept it, is to *I Spy* your way through your deck to arrive at confidential information about future-you. The path is not clear. Collect the clues to navigate your way and the operation will be a success.

For this activity use either a tarot deck or a tarot-based oracle deck for acceptable results. An oracle deck with detailed images and at least 50 cards should suffice as an alternative. After shuffling your cards, work from the top of your deck down, flipping one card at a time to fill in the adjacent pairs, based on the values given. Use the first card that has an item in it that fits the description but work in rows. So, if the even-numbered item appears first, place that card down and then continue to look for a card that can be matched for the odd number.

Put cards that do not apply into a discard pile, face up. One card should go in each place for row one, then move on to the second row and so on. If you run out of cards, flip over the discard pile, and start again using that. Do not reshuffle the deck. The gray spaces are for later.

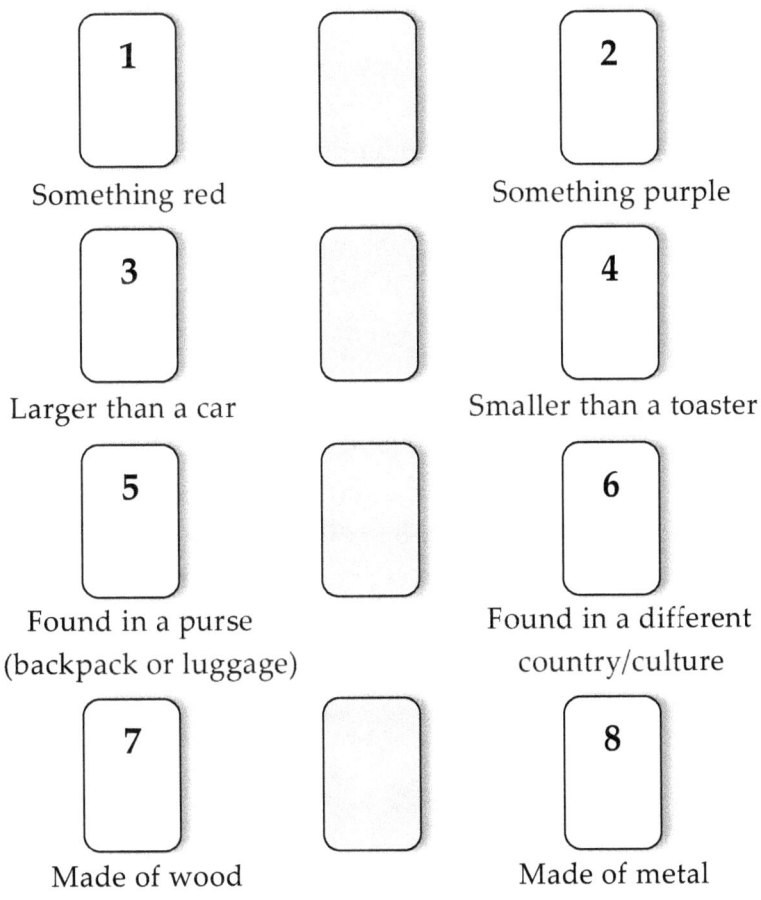

This is an excellent point to pause and diagram the layout in your notes. Leave room for adding information.

The Objects

Now having collected all eight cards, for the eight objects you spotted you should write notes that include a couple keywords to describe the meaning or symbolism. This is only about the individual eight objects, not the complete cards. Give precedence to your personal symbolism and what it makes you think of, but if you have a hard time with this, use one of the options from the resources section for ideas.

The Cards

After finishing those keyword notes, look at the overall cards and write a little about them as to the meaning. A general sentence or two per card is fine. Supplement your comments at the end if you wish.

Center Column

At this juncture, look at the pairing of cards in each row across. Choose one of the two cards and move it to the middle column. Try not to overthink this since you have not been given the purpose of it yet anyway. Leave the other cards in their original positions. When you have considered all four pairings and selected a center column, the next part of the activity is found in the No Peeking Section (page 176).

HIS. HER. THEIR.

It would be remiss to not include an exercise focused specifically on love and relationships. I would have it monogrammed for you if I could.

This special occasion calls for two decks. If you are in a love triangle, someone is out of luck. In the case of only having one deck, what you can do instead is shuffle your deck thoroughly, then split it into two relatively equal halves. Use each as individual decks for the next steps.

Whether you have two separate decks or two half-decks, determine which is going to represent you and which represents your significant other. The label of your relationship does not matter, only the connection between you. You may be kindred spirits, or conceivably kindred mates. One thing is undeniable, there is a soul agreement between you, as with all others you meet in life. This is the case whether meeting someone in passing or connecting to someone for a lifetime. If we think in terms of honoring these agreements, it gives us a better viewpoint.

Technically, if you want to address any other sort of relationship, such as between yourself and a sibling or co-worker, this will work for that sort of inquiry as well. Once you have used it, you will figure out how to make slight alterations to suit other applications.

FIRST STEP

Make three small scraps of paper with a heart, a moon, and a sun on them. Place them in any of the 12 positions where the cards will be laid out in the spread diagram on page 111. If you prefer, you can make a note of the assigned placements in your journal instead, such as "heart, 3; sun, 10; moon, 5." Do whichever is easiest for you. It only matters that this is pre-determined before laying out the cards.

Shuffle the deck you designated for yourself first. From the top card, count down your name to get to the cards you will use in the spread. For example, if your name is Kate, you would count down K-a-t-e and the fourth card is where you start. The cards removed from the top should be set face down in a discard pile above the spread; they are needed later. Lay out your cards face down for the left side; 1-2-5-6-9. Then, set your deck off to the left.

Add the other person's cards to the right side in the same way. Shuffle the deck you designated for them and use the letters of their name to get to the first card. The top unused cards go in the same discard pile with yours. Lay their cards in place, 3-4-7-8-10, and set that deck off to the right.

Now, take the cards in that top discard pile and fan them out, still face down. Select one to place in the 11 position and one for the 12 position. If you accidentally saw the cards, shuffle them before you fan them out.

The overview of the cards begins now, and with this number of cards it bodes well to take notes and journal before you move on to the No Peeking Section. Leave room between for adding comments about each card. To start, you should have at least two to three apparent keywords or phrases, along with symbols when you flip an individual card, and if you have a thought about the meaning, document it. Work in the order the cards are numbered, following the diagram, not the order you laid down the cards. That is, go straight through from 1 to 11. Remember that your heart, moon, and sun are connected to those three cards in there somewhere.

For the number 12 card, write the first two characteristics you are drawn to about the card and one keyword for each. You do not need to analyze any further on that. On to the Appendix now, page 146.

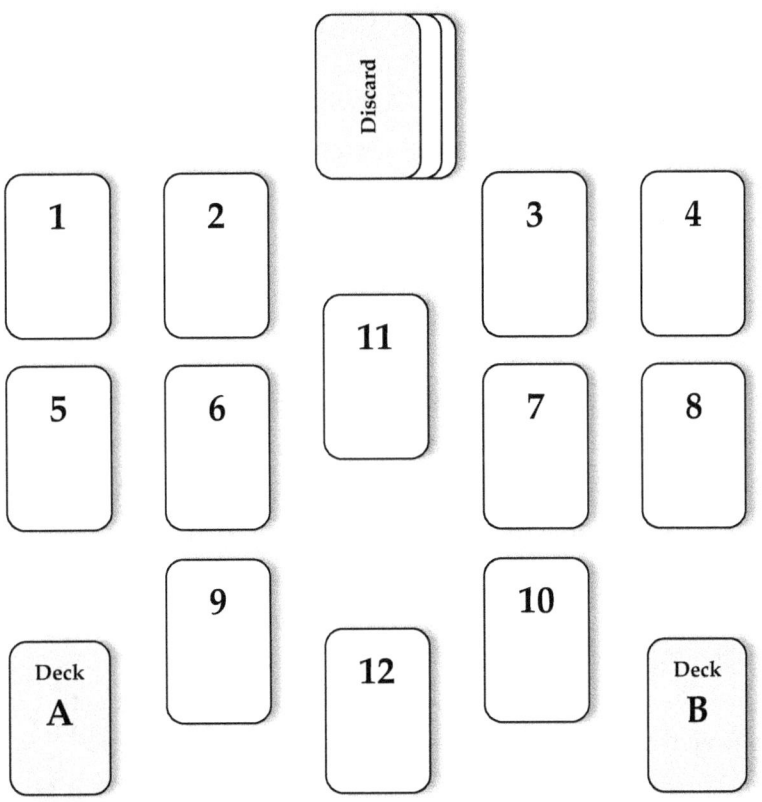

ART it UP

"Creative people are curious, flexible, persistent, and independent with a tremendous spirit of adventure and a love of play."
                                                            -Henri Matisse

A straightforward way to use tarot that people seldom consider is for creative inspiration. You may have already tried the acrostic, haiku, and lune poetic options in the book. All these activities were designed for tapping into your imaginative spirit. Some writers use their decks to sort out a plot detail or to find a missing personality trait for a character in development. This same resourcefulness adapts toward other pursuits, too.

In this instance, plan a solo project to work on using the exercise to get you started. The medium and application are entirely up to you. Artwork or creative pastimes of any genre apply: writing, music, crafting, building, baking, designing, gardening, dancing. Whatever sparks for you.

You will need your tarot deck and your journal for recording the information. That way you have the reference for when you begin your venture. To start, jot down the initial idea of what you would like to work on.

Give your deck a quick shuffle. As you do, ask for guidance on your project. A short list of card options is suggested. Before drawing cards, adapt the list to what is relevant to your respective plan. Clearly, if you are going to write a poem, you are not likely going to need the color scheme, but you could draw a card to ask for adjectives instead, prodigious adjectives. Try to only use five cards maximum so an overload of variables does not start to squelch your own imagination and process.

Suggested Card Values

Draw one card for a theme:

Draw one card for a mood:

Draw one card for a setting/atmosphere:

Draw one card for a focal color:

Color Palette:
(List key colors of all previous cards drawn.)

Once you have your cards and finish journaling, you are free to dabble and see where the inspiration takes you. Even if you veer away from what is deduced from the cards, chances are it gets your ingenuity firing. Know that any time you are at a crossroads with ideas, your deck may hold the answer, or at least will provide you several suggestions. Cheeky cards.

THE MISSING CARD

The major arcana of the tarot deck is meant to tell the story of a journey. It begins with the Fool setting off carefree, (or carelessly, depending on if he is upside down), until he reaches success (the World). Lay out all your major cards in order so you see how this is depicted in your own deck. There are people he runs into along the way, obstacles to overcome, bright spots that keep him moving along.

Before you begin, choose whether you want to attempt this activity seriously or with humor. Or, get settled in for a spell and try both versions. Either version will have you thinking creatively about your cards as you put trust in your inner voice and imagination.

FIRST ADD-IN

From a serious standpoint, a few deck creators opt to change traditional cards around like the devil becomes oppression, or death becomes transformation. Take it a step beyond this manner of change, however. Anyone can swap a synonym or change a card by drawing in a newt. Think along the lines of what life experience, meaning, interpretation, or archetypal person is absent from your deck. Is there a circumstance personal to you, a situation you have been through that does not seem to have any cards or characters to express this?

Create your own tarot card that you would add here. Between which two other cards should this missing card fall? Look at how the cards, on either side of the one you are inventing, keep the story arc going. Sketch your card, then write about its qualities. If you would like to invest more into it, include implications of the reversed card.

ITEMS	SYMBOLISM/KEYWORDS

Name of Card:	
Number of Card:	
Added Comments:	

SECOND ADD-IN

A sillier approach to this is to create a card that is all about making up a travel companion for the fool. You can decide if you are the fool starting out on the journey, or if the fool represents some other unsuspecting human for whom you will create a fictional sidekick.

This should not be entirely fluff. Give the new character a purpose and meaning for being there. What does this being add to the journey? Do they create a diversion? A delay? Do they impose their own agenda and what might that be? For this option, work in reverse of the last, writing your ideas down first and sketching second.

ITEMS	SYMBOLISM/KEYWORDS

TAROT GAMES

Name of Card:	
Number of Card:	
Added Comments:	

TAROT-for-TWO

This simple tarot activity is intended for two friends to do during a video chat, but it would work over a phone call. Both participants need to have their own tarot deck. It should never be done as a one-sided exercise; it is for balanced giving and receiving.

Ideally, choose to work with someone who has a like-minded approach regarding ethics of spirituality. This is the best way to ensure the exercise does not turn out lopsided. If it results in someone trying to stuff worms back into a can at the end, it was not done properly.

Begin by telling each other what your lucky number is, picking a number from 1 through 15. As you shuffle your decks, think, "What is it I want to tell my friend?" Instruct when to stop shuffling the decks. Both of you should cut your cards into three piles, left to right: one, two, three. Relay to each other in what order you want the other person's deck restacked.

Then, at the same time, use the friend's lucky number to select four cards, placing them in a horizontal line. So, if the friend's lucky number is six, take out every sixth card to make your row, and if your number is two, they take out every second card for theirs.

Decide who goes first and take turns going back and forth. After you explain your answers you may present the cards, or if on the phone describe them fully to help each other get the impression of the picture.

Card 1: "I see you."
Looking at the card, pick out one aspect of it that makes you think of your friend and articulate why. It does

not need to have anything to do with the card or general meaning of the card, traditional or otherwise. It may be about an object, the character, a color, the mood, motion, or the landscape. Approach the following cards in the same way, sharing a little story for each other to complete the sentence.

Card 2: "You are the best at…."

Card 3: "You are my friend because…."

Card 4: "My wish for you is…."

Keep your conversation going and talk about the cards that came up if you wish. When you try the activity again sometime, add on a fifth card of your own choosing, such as, "What I really appreciate about you is _____ ," or, "I hope someday we get to _____." Limit the cards to these few though, so there is extra time for chatting about other highpoints in life and let this be a discussion starter or closer.

If you enjoy working together, consider making the exercise a new tradition that you revisit on special occasions, as a way to celebrate birthdays or a favorite holiday, in a meaningful and nonmaterial way. You will learn more about your connection as new aspects are revealed. More than that, you get to keep sharing the love, building each other up.

WHEEL of COLORFUL FORTUNE

Give this insight activity a spin for a colorful take on tarot or try it with an oracle deck instead. One mention though, if you have several decks, avoid the original Rider-Waite, lest you become stuck in a primary color vortex with no options to escape. Select a deck with a broad color palette instead.

To begin, give your deck a good mix up, then fan the cards out in front of you, face down. You will be using the diagram below. If you wish, you can sketch it on a scrap of paper or an index card and put it as the center of the spread, so you do not have to keep referencing the book.

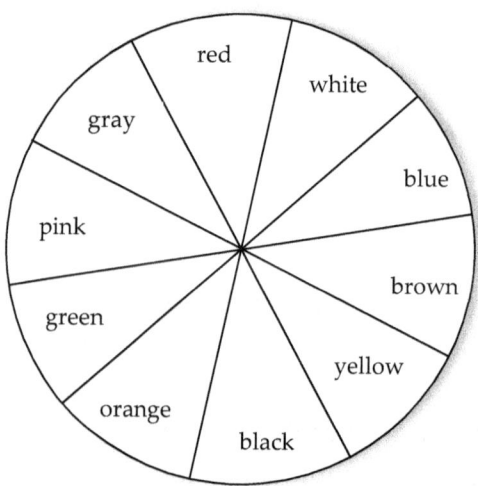

You will end up with five cards, drawing a card at a time. Choose one color visible in the card artwork, matching it to a space on the color wheel. There does not need to be any other reason for making the pairing. There are no incorrect results. Only one card may be placed on a color at a time. When you have your five cards selected, look them over and decide if you want to exchange one of the five. If so, you may swap out that one for a new card, placing it on any of the open colors. Stand by your decision. If you opt to make the trade, you cannot revert. Discard the one you exchanged back to the fanned deck.

When you have your final set of five, explanations about the card values are in the No Peeking Section of the Appendix (page 192).

EXTRA OPTIONS

If you want to do a speed round, you can just as easily do this activity drawing fewer cards. A single card would be a fine option for a message-of-the-day.

Every time you give the wheel a spin with your cards, it creates a brand-new tarot spread. Unless you choose only the same colors repeatedly, that is. Keep it in mind for the next time you want a personalized set of insights.

SKETCHY TOO

If you enjoyed the first *Sketchy* exercise in the activities section, we have another version of that to try, this time adding a twist of tarot to it. Once again, you need a blank journal page or other paper to draw on with a pen, pencil, or marker. Do leave plenty of time for this activity as it is a longer one. It begins with your sketching activity and drawing evaluation, followed by the Tell Me More tarot spread. With the drawing, general realizations are brought to light. By adding the layer of tarot to it, it illuminates your exact situation.

Draw the items in the list according to the order and instructions below. You may sketch them however you wish aside from that.

> **Subjects**
> Choose one or two:
> A garden, A desert, A mountain
>
> Add one:
> A cabin, A hot air balloon, A cactus
>
> Then include these three:
> A man
> A bunny
> A bee

Complete your entire sketch before moving on to the next part in the Appendix (page 153).

SNAPSHOT

Tarot is always one snapshot in time based on the moment of the reading. Asking about the past allows for hindsight that may shift understanding. When inquiring about the future, it reveals potentials. A million decisions, thoughts and ideas manifesting, free will, other people's free will, world events, *everything* plays into the intricacies of what ultimately comes together. A myriad of layers constructs our experiences, energies overlapping and intertwining. It makes every day malleable as it originates. The future certainly is not set in stone.

This tarot game is for a snapshot in time, too. Set the intention over a timeframe first. It should depend on if you want to study how life is now, in the near future, in the distant future, or in the past. Choosing the past as your focus applies if you need to reflect on a matter that is behind you. If looking ahead, what is presented is meant to bring information forth so that you can decide for yourself how to proceed, how to manifest, or how to improve a part of life. Though, on a belligerent day, it could result in how to suppress progress or further avoid a challenge.

Peeking at what is to come is not going to show absolutes. Nor will it give away mysteries that would go against your interest. For those who say, "But I do not want to know what is coming." That is not how metaphysics works. Ever. Not tarot, not psychic readings, not any form of divination. You will not "know your future," because you are still creating it. What does happen is that the soul may permit access to limited information, for the intention of empowerment in manifesting. It is up to you to decide how to apply, adjust, and navigate.

1. **Set intention** for (past, present, near future, distant future): _____
2. **Take four pictures** of four different objects around you. If you want, allow added time with this, and take four meaningful pictures through the course of the day. Then, finish the exercise in the evening.
3. **Label the photos**. These are your symbols. For example, if you first took a picture of an *old, green shoe,* that would be your label.

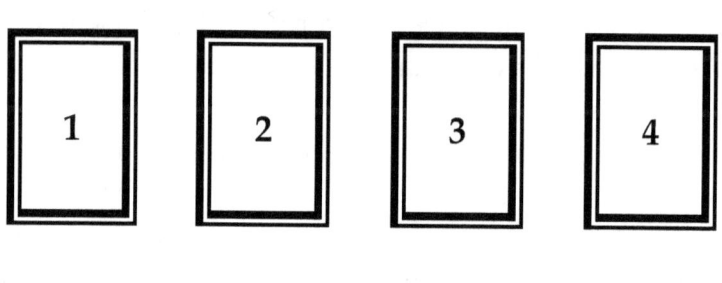

_____   _____   _____   _____

On to your cards. A tarot deck is necessary for this activity. Shuffle the cards well. Cut the deck if you like. Then, as you prefer, either fan out the deck and select one card at a time, or work from the top of your deck down to using cards sequentially as they are stacked.

Draw and discard until you have one card of each suit. You must keep the first in each suit that appears.

    First pentacles card:
    First wands card:
    First cups card:
    First swords card:

Which order to place these four cards in is shown when you advance to the next step. Find this in the Appendix on page 172.

THROUGH a TELESCOPE

To wrap up the tarot section, a full tarot spread as a reward for all your work on these activities is precisely the right way to celebrate. It is a look through a telescope to find out all about you. While intended for use with tarot, an oracle deck may be used.

If you want to zhuzh it up, go wild and use both a tarot and an oracle deck (or two tarot decks). For a doubled version, after you go through the instructions for the first deck, repeat the process with the second so you have a pair of cards in each spot.

Think as you shuffle, "Enlighten me about myself." When you are happy with your deck, count down from the top card to your favorite number. That is card one, which is the center of the spread. Place the cards face down to start. You will see them soon enough.

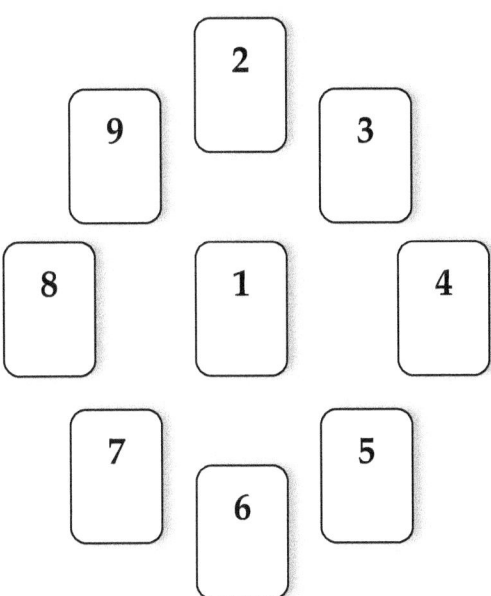

The unused cards from the top of the deck or decks may be set aside into a discard pile. Fill positions two through nine, in a clockwise circle with cards directly underneath that favorite number. If you are going for the double-up version with two decks, now is the time to repeat the layout with the second deck.

Mind you, the notion to use two decks is all in fun. It *is* extra work to interpret. If you are hesitant, skip it. It will be there to try another time. An overload of cards does not mean better results. In fact, this frequently is a red flag. When you see people who "read tarot," consistently using layers upon layers of cards, decks upon decks, it only means they are using them as filler and flash. They are not actually connecting with higher sources of wisdom. It is made to look like they are, reciting memorized bits of generalized text, multiplied by all the cards they have on display, but it is akin to Miss Cleo's scripts.

A person who practices authentic psychic tarot spends little time flipping cards and all the time tuning into using their ultra-sensory abilities. Each card having a purpose and a value within the spread, like you see in any reliable book written about tarot. The person does not need a sea of cards to be able to elaborate on them for the querent.

If you know a little bit about the cards, that frees you up to hear your inner voice. The truest cognizance comes from that place within yourself. The cards then become artwork to illustrate your intuited story, as they were created to do.

But for now, back to your telescope.

Write a few keywords and brief notes about the cards, turning one over at a time. Catch that first card aspect you see and remark on the symbolism. You can supplement comments later once you have the values of the cards.

When you focus on one at a time it is easier to concentrate, and then once they are all turned over, look at the overall picture to see if there are other highlights. It ordinarily happens that you see a theme through the colors, imagery that parallels between cards, characters that are connected, and such.

Upon finishing your observations, continue to the No Peeking Section (page 189) to see the meanings and make additional notes.

For anyone who has wondered why all the values for these exercises are split into the Appendix, there is a reason for not seeing them first, of course. The idea is that in trying all the tarot activities, when you observe your cards and learn to pay attention to the symbolism on your own, you develop faith in your inner voice. If you see connotations assigned to the cards first, then limitation, parameters, and expectation are set. It becomes too easy to rely on the generic meanings, skipping over what your heart is telling you.

If you have kept to the plan and stuck to the directions, you have taken full advantage of these activities. While they were created in a lighter manner, there were greater workings going on all along, for the sake of alignment to your true soul self. Keep exploring as you revisit practices in the book. Give yourself credit for the progress you make because heightened awareness does take diligence.

Venture on into the following section on meditations and enjoy further opportunities for expanding your magic.

PART THREE
MEDITATIONS

ONE OF THE BEST OPTIONS FOR CULTIVATING HIGHER awareness is to practice ultra-sensory meditation. Once proficient, you can do it anytime, anywhere you want. For a minute to relax or an hour to explore, there are immeasurable possibilities. Through this effort it is possible to access insight, guidance, and healing by elevating perception to function at a heightened frequency. In doing so, it activates all the senses, enabling easier communication between human consciousness and soul self. There is a potential to connect with spirit guides and Divine wisdom, as well.

For a paced introduction, the four-step tutorial in *Through the Blue Door* is advantageous, both for those who have never done meditation and those who want a refresher.

Working one by one through the sensory abilities as they are applied in meditation, you learn what to expect firsthand, practicing as you go.

The handful of choices in this section are a sampler of what may be experienced with meditation. One thing people do not always realize is that meditating does not have to be approached solemnly every time. It is no wonder the misunderstanding, with the circulating photographs of serene models in their tropical sunrise paradises deep into lotus poses, seemingly miles from civilization. How many people have looked at one of those photographs and thought, "Pass. My knees have not bent that way since 1999." Surprise! There are no mandatory ingredients for successful meditation. Yoga is yoga. Meditation is meditation. If you combine the two, fantastic, but meditation is its own pursuit. Merge it with competitive ice cream eating, even that can work.

Anyone can meditate. Unless a person tells himself he cannot. While that is self-fulfilling, deciding so is only a sign of fear or being uninvested in knowing their true self. It has nothing to do with the feasibility of meditation, however. Apart from that, if someone believes they cannot meditate without a floor cushion, Spandex, and an ocean view, or for that matter, incense, candles, and new age music, they have done themselves a disservice. It is not as troubling as those with hostility toward stillness though.

I never heard a person who learned to meditate express regret about it. Sincerely, sit how you are comfortable, in a place you can relax for a moment. No excuses. Do not empty your mind. Listen. *Observe.* Let thoughts, imagery, and feelings come to you. Give it a go. These guided meditations will help you set an objective to focus on.

SOUNDTRACKED AGAIN

Our soul self sees it all. Surely, there is no judgment. No matter how many times it takes for a concept to sink in here. But what if that whole of us were to tell it like it is for a moment? It would probably amount to a roast, party of one. We can soften the candor a notch with another musical message instead.

Soundtracked Again is a meditation combined with the earlier music exercise. CDs or a vinyl album selection works for this. You can use another music source instead if you prefer, all you need to do is adapt the rules a smidge.

This starts with asking, "Self, what two songs are the soundtrack for my life right now?" Find the first by taking out the album corresponding to the number that comes to mind, then ask for which number song. Give a quick listen or read through the lyrics.

When you are ready to meditate, relax by continuing to play this song through in your mind as you drift into meditative state. Imagine as you focus on the song, that the dark setting lightens enough to find yourself in a venue where your first song gives way to the second song. This location is specific to you. Stay as long as you wish there to listen to your music, and if you have questions, try asking for clarity.

It is a superb idea to ask for validation of the songs at the end. See what happens in the days following. This is one way to keep the conversation and mindfulness flowing.

Anytime you wish for a refreshed soundtrack and advice, all you must do is revisit the meditation.

EWE LLAMA IGUANA

Meditations do not have to be about solving all the problems of the Universe, they can purely be about repose and pleasantness. What is better than connecting with an animal to bring calm, humor, or a big dose of adorable? Forget about the drama of the day by visiting a llama. Step out of the routine and pat a platypus or hug a koala. All you need is to let your mind be open.

Approach this either intending to drop in on an animal sanctuary or deciding to let the setting reveal itself. The same applies to the animals. If there is one that you would be partial to interact with, ask for that to happen. If you are open to surprises, go into it with no plan. There is likely to be at least one other person in the scene guiding you. Sit with your animal, walk around with it, feed it a treat. Ask if there is a name to call it by or name it yourself. It is up to you to spend your time there how you wish.

If you did not pre-determine the animal or animals you saw, ask if there is a special reason or symbolic meaning behind which ones appear.

Leave with an expression of gratitude. When you have finished with your meditation, if you would like, check to see if your animal is listed in the Animal Symbolism Guide (page 197). There may be additional insight you find within the animal wisdoms there.

UP PERISCOPE

If you completed any other activity in the book and want better understanding of the results or found that questions arose from what was learned, try this meditation. It works with other life matters, too.

Here is a go-to option for increasing knowledge or getting a second opinion from your wiser, higher self. Perplexed about love? Dithering over a job offer? Meditation takes you out of your mind-space where the chaos and lies fester and moves you into your heart-space so you can get to your truth. Access a source energy level of meditative consciousness where there is not expectation, force, or control, but observation, connection, and faith.

Once you are settled in and ready to begin, think about the topic or situation you want to address and try to land on a single request. "I would like to understand about ____," as an example. Once you have asked, put yourself into a listening and observational mode, by first concentrating on your pattern of breaths. Allow that to draw you deeper into meditative state, until you are ready to focus your vision. The place you find as your setting will be somewhere that is known or familiar to you in some way, but with one difference. There is a large pod that has been temporarily placed there for you. Certain to vary from person to person, the pod may appear as a science-fiction style enclosure, or a storage cube, or an oversized playhouse. Let it be whatever it may be. It is entertaining to see what turns up.

Look for the entrance and go on in. You may nose around a bit to let your senses adjust, in order to focus at an intensified level. As you do this, notice there are a few different periscope apparatuses set up. Look through whichever ones you wish, in any order. Each will give you a raised and varied viewpoint about your situation. The new perspectives work to identify facts about the issue and hopefully bring resolution to your question. When you are done viewing, address questions while still in the pod. Cover concepts that you were confused by or new questions that arose.

When you exit, the pod vanishes. For some, the setting may have a bigger importance, and if so, do not feel rushed to end the meditation. You can undoubtedly spend some of the time investigating the scene and unwind awhile. Either way, your scene fades behind you as you decide to conclude your meditation.

LIKE MAGIC

"The Universe is full of magical things patiently waiting for our wits to grow sharper."   -Eden Phillpots

Another amazing facet of meditation is being able to venture into scenes and settings that range from inaccessible to unearthly or supernatural. Right now, it is time to visit your very own wizarding world.

MEDITATIONS

Before zapping yourself through the consciousness portal into meditation, decide what question or topic has been on your mind lately. It could be a personal or family issue, or a current event. As easily, you could pick a subject matter that interests you to learn about. To set the intention for wisdom, concepts, and info to come to you, write the idea you land on at the top of a page in your journal. Have your tarot deck on hand for later.

Ease into your meditation, allowing the darkness as you relax and listen to your breathing. Let that draw your attention into higher frequencies until ready to proceed. At that point, the light starts to filter in on your setting.

Get to your otherworldly destination by whatever mode of transportation is awaiting you when your meditative vision comes in to focus.

A gregarious shopkeeper lurks around somewhere to assist with any needs once you arrive. When you first find this person, or better chance of them finding you honestly, tell them you are there to find the *tarot keys*. A satchel will be given to you for carrying these keys. They may guide you around or at least give instruction to get you started. From there, you must wander their shop and possibly around the village, to locate and collect your tarot keys. There may be symbolic messages along the way, so if high points of your adventure draw your attention, make note of this so you can analyze it at the end.

These are not just ordinary keys you are searching for, however. The individual "keys" you want are designed as coins, knives, goblets, and magic wands. Only one of the four varieties may show up, but feasibly a combination. You must keep track of the quantity, as there will be anywhere from zero to ten of each.

When you are done gathering your tarot keys, you have the option to make one additional stop along the way at the hidden alleyway entrance to a secret locale. Here you can put in a request for a thought, wish, desire, or an idea you would like to manifest. Put a little extra magic to work for you.

Thank the shopkeeper guide while having them direct you back to your ride home. Once you hop on, take a fast inventory of how many of each type of key you have. Let yourself close your eyes on the scene and return your focus back to breathing, which helps transport you back to the physical world.

Back alert at home now, you should record the tarot key count in your journal and write about your experience. Then, using your tarot deck, sort through to find the minor arcana cards that pair with the tarot keys you found. For instance, if you found two goblets and nine coins, you would take out the two of cups and the nine of pentacles.

Interpret your cards in relationship to your initial question or topic and add your findings to the journal entry. Come back to this meditation whenever you are up for another enchanted adventure.

ELEMENTALITY

It is only appropriate to combine awareness activity, tarot, and meditation into one for this final task. Leave expectation behind for an adventuresome study.

MEDITATIONS

Beginning by shuffling your deck, think to yourself, "Which element is beneficial for me to explore today?" By whatever means you wish, draw a single card to find your element. They are represented traditionally by the suits. Pentacles for earth; swords for air, wands for fire, and cups for water. Add to that spirit, which for this exercise should apply to any major arcana card drawn. When you have that, you also have your corresponding shape based on the element. Earth is represented by a square. Air is a circle. Fire is a triangle. Water is a droplet and Spirit is a star. Use the picture on page 138 for a reference.

The meditation begins like the others, relaxing and letting tension dissipate as you listen to your rhythm of inhaling and exhaling. In the darkness of the meditative state, allow your vision to adjust and imagine that your shape appears as a colorful light ahead of you. Focusing on this, it broadens into an energetic doorway that you may pass through for a spectacular elemental experience. How much time you spend in observation and contemplation is entirely up to you. It may be possible to telepathically communicate with your higher self while there if you have questions about what you are seeing and what you are meant to know about it. When you are ready to finish, step back through the shaped portal. It swirls closed behind you. Allow the light to fade and your consciousness to return you home.

Keep track of your elemental adventures in your journal and soon you will be able to compare all five types. Check over the initial card you drew to see if added value comes from the card meaning or imagery following the meditation. There is a chance it contains a validating sign that you encounter in the few days following.

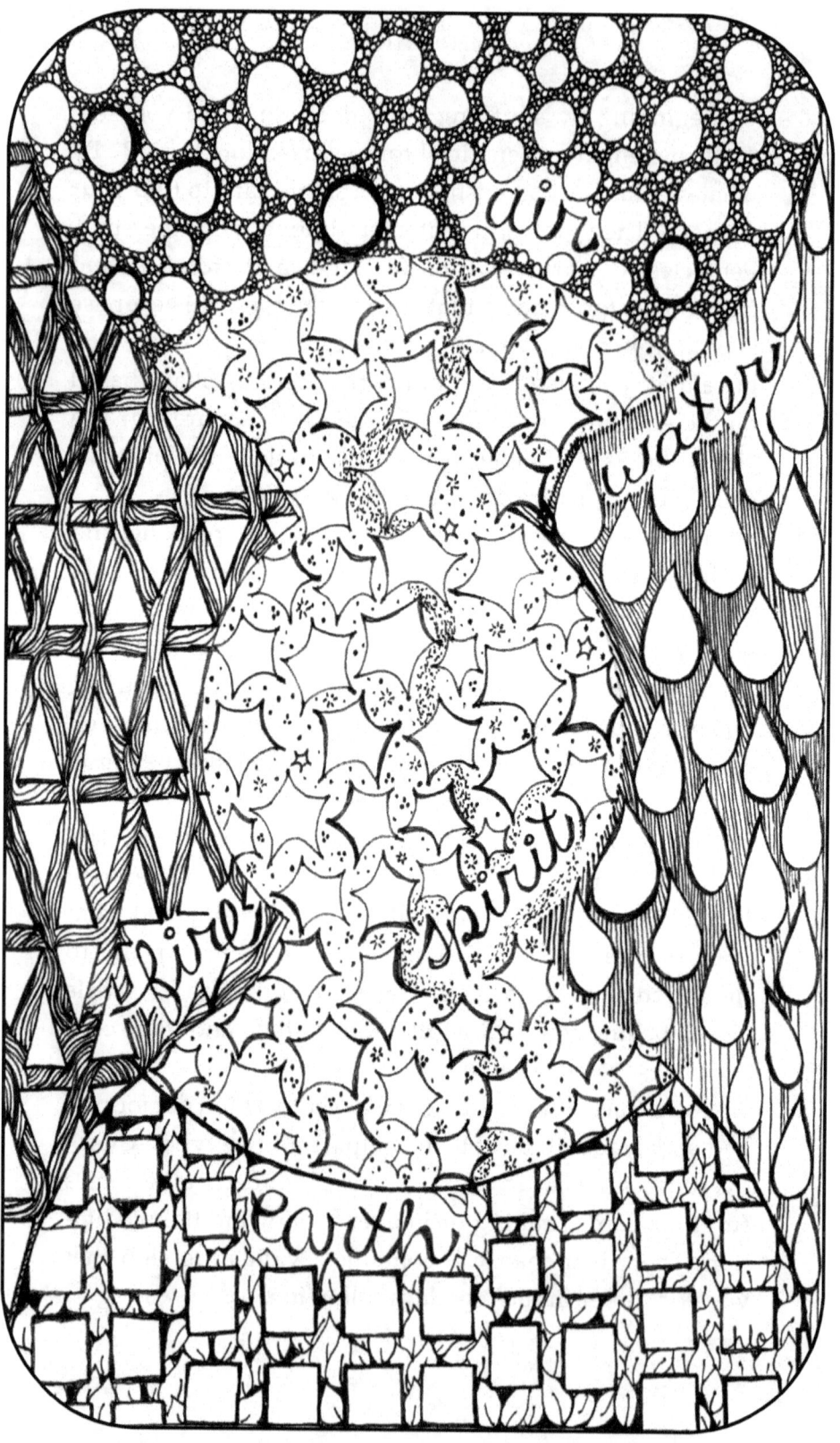

PART FOUR
Appendix

CONTENTS

No Peeking Section	**141**
Beside Myself Results	142
Color Me Cured Results	144
His. Her. Their. Interpreting the Cards	146
Lune-a-Day Themes	148
Photojournalist on the Prowl: Part Two	149
Sign of the Times Messages	152
Sketchy Too Drawing Interpretation	153
Tell Me More Tarot	169
Affirmation	171
Reading for Yourself	171
Snapshot Symbolism	172
Tarot Spy: Part Two	174
Tarot Spy Mission: Top Secret	178
Tarot Spy Solitaire Part Two	179
Tarot Zoo Continued	180
Part Two: Interpreting the Cards	180
Part Three: The Animal Signs	183
That's a Little Sketchy Evaluation	184
Through a Telescope Card Values	189
Times are a-Changin' Interpretation	190
Wheel of Colorful Fortune Values	192
Bonus	193
Word-Fill to Find Insight Solution	194
Animal Symbolism Guide	**197**
Helpful Resources	201
An Afterword	202
About the Author	207
Art Prints	207
Notes	208

NO PEEKING SECTION

In this section of the Appendix find follow-up answers, solutions, and additional steps for the activities and games. Avoid flipping through these pages until you complete the previous steps and are ready to finalize the activity on which you are working.

All exercises here are in alphabetical order.

☙ SPOILER ALERT ☙

Read beyond this page only to complete activities started on preceding pages.

BESIDE MYSELF Results

Prioritize the moment using your winning pile of guidance. Use the suggestion corresponding with your pile, or a similar version based on your personal life and interests. Distract yourself with this for a spell and do not worry. You have got this.

Pile 1: Make a phone call. Write a letter. Send a card or care package. Reach out and connect with someone you have been thinking about. This option spreads joy and benefits you both.

Pile 2: Get a little work done. This may be job-related, or it could be completing a household chore or trying a new recipe. Still feeling discombobulated? Choose a five-minute task. Those foster ideas.

Pile 3: Spend some time on a passion or hobby. It does not matter what it is; let some of what is inside you come out. You are a creative being. Do not forget it. Not sure what your talents are? Listen to music, compare songs, and decide which is your favorite. Take a virtual tour of a museum, start an online class, or follow a tutorial on a craft. Be inspired.

Pile 4: Read a book. About anything. Escape for a bit. Or explore a new idea. Not sure where to begin? Look into ley lines, ancient ruins, quantum physics, or dream symbols. Wise up, not dumb down. Get away from the trivial junk people want to dump on others and dig into a topic you genuinely want to know about. All for *you*.

Pile 5: It is time to do some planning. Apply this however you like. Organize your tax receipts or pay some bills if that thrills you. Check on your investments or look into investing. Or, plan a dream vacation or a party for no reason. There is a vision board with your name on it. Go fill it up.

If you used a detailed tarot deck, you may want to look through the five cards in your result pile to see if there are additional messages for you to take away or to use as the foundation for a meditation. The intention there is that they give you messages and clues as to what is in your best interest. A card in a negative light is likely about blockages and resistance or is the indication of a delay. If you need more insight on your cards, follow with meditation, such as Up Periscope, to help make sense of what you are trying to interpret.

Need something else to work with? Play the Traveling Wilburys, *End of the Line* and dance it out.

COLOR ME CURED Results

This is a reminder to take your results with a grain of salt. If it feels right to you, then you can use them. No one is trying to muck about with your free will. If you were not confident in your choices, or if you felt the results were hazy and you ended up settling and picking a color, then realize it is better to try it again another day, rather than force it to be "correct."

Some people, *most people,* never devote time toward developing awareness of their ultra-sensory ability to have confidence in it. If the exercise felt easy, that is remarkable. If you did not feel anything happening, it is not abnormal; it reflects your baseline for enhancement. Should it interest you, look into energetic self-awareness and intuition studies, such as the *Presence of Light* workshop series.

So, on to the results.

Feels Worst Today

For the color you labeled Feels Worst Today, look at the representation in the Color Key. Identify if this is something that feels lacking or off-balance. If so, try this suggestion first. Watch for an energy-stabilizing effect.

If it does not feel lacking but aversive, then put it aside for now and let divine timing lead you to attend to it when it is important. Instead, skip to the Feels Best Today part.

The reason for the dual possibilities is that in doing this activity, people tend to perceive energy in different ways, so the options are an attempt to guide those who fall into separate groups as to what is best for them.

Feels Best Today

For the color that you labeled Feels Best Today, try the associated activity from the Color Key after you do the suggestion for "worst." If you skipped straight to this part, this will be your only suggested option.

In either situation, pay attention to how your energy feels before and after. Does it give you a boost? How are your emotions shifted? If you are so inclined to journal about your energy awareness through this activity, spend a few minutes doing this.

COLOR KEY

Black	Rest. Catnap soon or do what is needed right now in preparation for getting a good sleep tonight. (Back away from the caffeine, spicy food, and screens.)
Blue	Connect with someone. Call or video chat with a family member or friend if you cannot meet face-to-face.
Green	Eat a nutritious food. Listen to your body to find the right healthy snack or meal.
Orange	Drink more water. Now.
Purple	Engage your mind. Read a book. Watch a documentary. Find a new topic to learn about. Try an activity on your bucket list.
Red	Exercise. Take a walk. Dance around. Get in a full-fledged workout. It is up to you; get moving like no one is watching.
Yellow	Quick energy boost with an affirmation. "I am happy, healthy, and aligned to pure source energy." Or, your own version of that.

HIS. HER. THEIR. Interpreting the Cards

As you go through the card interpretations, attentive to the assigned values, add comments to your notes.

1: What you have to offer to the relationship
2: What you want to receive from the relationship
3: What the other person has to offer
4: What the other person wants to receive
5: What is stuck in your head (holds you back)
6: What is pulling at your heart (urges you forward)
7: What is stuck in their head (holds them back)
8: What is pulling at their heart (urges them forward)

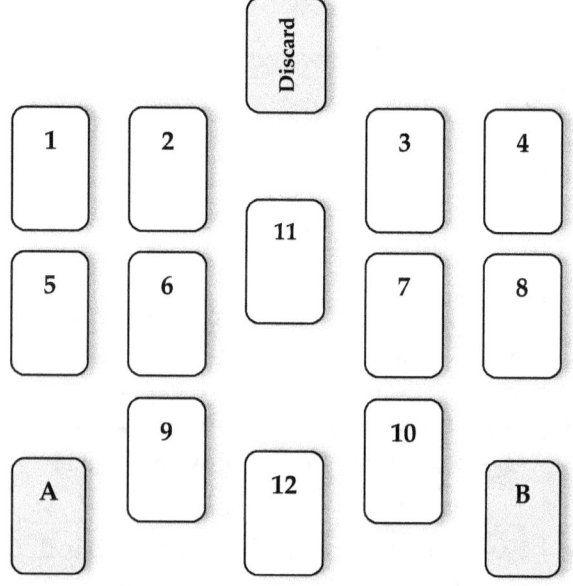

9: How you honor the soul agreement between you
10: How they honor the soul agreement between you
11: A message about your future together

NO PEEKING SECTION

Now for the mysterious 12th card and a *hidden message.* For this you need to look up a couple of "puzzle pieces." Find the last message, email, or text you *sent* to the other person and write down the first word and last word of the message. Next, add to that the first word and last word of the most recent message you *received* from this person.

Add these four words to the two keywords you wrote earlier on. Piece this together into a short sentence revealing your hidden message. Of course, if it is needed, add in other words to assemble it in a way that makes sense, but try to use as few extras as possible.

For some, it may result in hidden messages between your higher selves. In one case, the keywords *love* and *awaken* were added to communication words, *I*, *I'm*, *worth*, and *sorry*. The hidden message resulted as two short sentences, *"I am worthy of love,"* and *"I'm sorry; I am trying to awaken."*

The last pieces of this puzzle are those three secret signs, the heart, moon, and sun.

 Look at the card you placed on the heart. Within the card is a symbol that will be sent to you as a sign of love.

 The card placed on the moon contains a clue about an unknown aspect of the relationship that will be brought to light. It may involve an opportunity, blessings, or abundance.

 A clue about your next adventure within the relationship is hiding in the card you paired to the sun. It may involve a big decision, travel, family, or a shared endeavor.

LUNE-a-DAY Themes

There is not a follow-up to this activity, but in case you did try guessing the answers to the themes for the lune samples, you can check to see if you were accurate. The answers are in order as they were shown.

Good news arriving: Eight of Wands
Tangible progress: Knight of Pentacles
Twist of fate: Wheel of Fortune
Wield big talent: Three of Pentacles

NO PEEKING SECTION

PHOTOJOURNALIST on the PROWL:
Part Two

**Try to not skip and read ahead or go out of order, as that may alter your responses in some way.

Your photo sequence corresponds with the second part of this activity. Imagine a single picture is a snapshot of one aspect of the week ahead. With each representation, write a few notes in your journal about the symbolism or immediate thoughts about them before you move on to the next photo. Write an overall summary at the end. Revisit this at the end of the weeks' time to add any clarifying notes or validation.

PHOTO ONE represents your individual outlook, mood, or motivation for the week. Description of photo:

Symbolism, personal meaning, initial thoughts:

PHOTO TWO represents another person who will be a part of your week; a situation to be aware of ahead of time regarding your interactions. Description of photo:

Symbolism, personal meaning, initial thoughts:

PHOTO THREE represents your innermost inspiration, your purpose and keeping on track. Description of photo:

Symbolism, personal meaning, initial thoughts:

PHOTO FOUR represents matters of practicality, responsibilities, and obligations. Description of photo:

Symbolism, personal meaning, initial thoughts:

PHOTO FIVE represents means of change, growth, transformation, or learning. Description of photo:

Symbolism, personal meaning, initial thoughts:

OVERALL, the week ahead:

CONCLUSION

Now that the week is finished, I want to add:

SIGN of the TIMES Messages

Once you have received your sign and are confident in that, find your animal below and read your corresponding message. In all likelihood, it has arrived at exactly the right time that you need to hear it.

Retain that animal as a sign between you and your guides if you feel a connectivity in it. If you wish to, try again with another animal. In that case, refrain from reading through the entire list of responses below, or wait until you have forgotten the words if it was unavoidable.

These are typical words of encouragement our higher selves and spirit guides try to send us. Most commonly they relay simple statements meant to nudge us ahead, calm us down, or remind us who we are.

Chimpanzee
Observe. Slow down.
Be still.

Dolphin
You are not ever alone.
You are loved.

Lion
Remember that divine timing is working in your favor. Be patient.

Penguin
You are doing great.
Keep going. Results or blessings will follow.

Rabbit
Get outside to breathe in fresh air.
Restore balance.

Wolf
Focus on the now.
Be in the moment.
Do not miss out.

NO PEEKING SECTION

SKETCHY TOO Drawing Interpretation

In reference to your completed drawing, look only for the subject listings on the following pages that correspond. This is more intricate than your first Sketchy, so it requires some patience as you browse. Find the pertinent descriptions to help interpret your drawing. Bypass parts that are not relevant. If a meaning is unclear, the later tarot portion may bring personalized insight. The subjects are covered in the order they were listed.

A GARDEN

If you chose the garden, this is about life's abundance and personal spirituality. How this is for you is reflected by how lush the garden is that you drew. If it is filled with plants and blossoming flowers, it correlates to life being on track. Hard work is paying off and rewards will come.

A **sparse, weedy, or unplanted** garden is telling of true abundance that you have not yet experienced. There may be struggles with manifesting blessings lately. Attending to spiritual self-care would be beneficial toward putting you back on track soon. One small change or effort is all it takes to create a wave of progress and new growth begins.

Should the garden take up the **width of your page**, abundance is meant to come as it is clearly of importance to you. This speaks to persevering through hard times; keep trying and giving attention to your spiritual self.

If the garden is **quite small** on the page, there may be resistance or confusion to overcome regarding spiritual growth. If you do not know where to begin, realize you are doing exactly that, through the activities in the book. Do not be so hard on yourself.

In the event your garden has a **gate or clear entrance**, it is a sign of a wonderful, fortuitous event on the horizon.

A DESERT

If you drew a desert, it is about independence, isolation, and solitude, and the wisdom that comes only by living through these life experiences. How this applies is dependent on the appearance of the desert.

A desert that has **hills, dunes, and wavy lines** is about triumphing through one's independence or single life. Seeing life as an adventure worth exploring. Using time of independence to fulfill your life purpose, not sacrificing it to someone else.

If there is an **absence of all life** (except those subjects you were given to add to the drawing), and if the desert is one flat line, it is about independence or single life bringing a feeling of loneliness. It may similarly represent feelings of isolation or loneliness despite being surrounded by others. Shift perspective to see the purpose and opportunities bestowed, rather than viewing lack.

A **dry and cracked** desert represents feelings of a forced isolation or solitary life, such as through a death, divorce, health issue, or other circumstance that prohibits an intimate partnership. Heal resentment or hopelessness. From there, dedication to individual purpose is key.

If the desert only **takes up a small portion** of the picture, it is saying you recognize that this is only part of your life experience story. It represents independence gained through living on one's own (single, single parent, widow). This is time for personal growth and/or healing, possibly in preparation for a quality relationship with an equal.

Excluding adding the subjects on the list, if you drew any **extra feature in the desert** apart from sand, distinguishing it as a desert, it shows that a time of loneliness is about to change or improve. There are surprises yet to come. Now is your chance to focus on actively manifesting what you want the next phase of your life to be.

A MOUNTAIN

If you opted to draw a mountain, this represents life's journey of knowledge and higher awareness. Central to this, are the challenges we intended to encounter as part of our life plan. How this applies is dependent upon the appearance of the mountain and the following details.

If your mountain takes up the **width of your page**, it is about oppressive feelings, worrying about what is to come in the future. It shows fear surrounding a challenge (or a number of challenges, if multiple peaks) which may or may not exist yet. There may be doubts and concerns held about the unknown aspects of the future. Constructive techniques for focusing on present tasks and goals and living in the moment are useful. This discourages the manifestation of terrible obstacles.

When the mountain is **small in proportion** to the size of the whole drawing, and if the other components are the same size or larger than the mountain, there is a message regarding being observant. Do not be careless about or oblivious to a challenge as it may catch you off-guard. Not to worry, but to engage in preparedness. In a worst-case scenario, it would represent willful ignorance or general disrespect toward a life situation. It may be time to re-evaluate.

If your mountain is a **range of mountains** in the background, it would represent a typical way of looking at life. This is about knowing there are challenges to be faced, yet carrying the confidence in having the skills to get through whatever anything; taking life as it comes.

For a mountain that has only **one peak**, shown off in the background, it would represent a concern that is growing or will need to be faced in the future. Keep an eye on the situation; trust you will know when to make a decision.

But if a single-peak mountain appears in the foreground or to one side, it is representative of a situation you are already aware of or dealing with; you have the knowledge to handle it.

If the mountain has **trees** on it, you know that the situation or challenge is bringing about growth, whether or not it is hard work to go through. Higher awareness guides you and increases by having this life experience.

If the mountain is **snow-capped**, it represents emotional detachment from a situation, whereas if there is running water or a waterfall on the mountain, it is showing that while it may be an emotional situation to go through, you are not repressing feelings, but handling it as best you can.

A mountain that is **rocky** shows that you have strength and endurance through a trying time.

A GARDEN + A DESERT

If you chose both a garden and desert for your picture, it represents a duality in life, a balance between pleasure and endeavor. Always striving and persevering, not avoidant of change or challenge, granted it is a healthy garden. It may also speak to prioritizing higher knowledge, a lifelong quest to learn. Alternatively, if the garden is weedy, minimal in size to the desert, and/or empty, that speaks to a disparity and imbalance instead.

When a garden is depicted **growing in a desert**, it may represent reward coming after a major life obstacle. The good that transpires from enduring tragedy, grief, or loss.

If the garden drawn was intended to be **an oasis**, there is a situation in life to be evaluated for its authenticity. If it is real, it will be amazing. If it is not genuine, discern if your soul is trying to make you aware of what you truly want, then you can do what is needed to invite that into your life.

A DESERT + A MOUNTAIN

For a drawing with the combination of a desert and a mountain, it indicates having to face a situation alone. Or, feeling like you must go through it on your own, regardless of whether others are there or are offering support.

If the mountain is a **barren part of the desert** it may be showing that it feels like there is no end in sight to certain circumstances. Discouraging thoughts or pessimism may be draining a higher perspective. It may simply be time for a change; invite the opportunity.

If the mountain is a **verdant contrast to the desert**, it shows there is hope. A potential for transformation is coming, if you are willing to take the chance.

A MOUNTAIN + A GARDEN

In the case of a mountain drawn along with a garden, it represents a natural continuity and flow in life, being able to go with whatever comes your way. You may carry the optimism that no matter what happens today, tomorrow is a brand-new day.

When the garden and mountain are **spaced separately**, far apart in the picture, is implies something standing in the way of accepting your spiritual whole. Worrying what others think or dismissing your wishes and interests to prioritize someone else's are two examples. Overcome what stands in the way to become an unstoppable force for good.

If the garden (assuming it is a healthy one) is **at the foot of the mountain or surrounding it**, your higher consciousness and life purpose are aligning. Continue to be receptive. Your soul knows the way.

A CABIN

Including the cabin choice in your drawing carries symbolism of your personal autonomy and indicates its importance at this time. How it appears mirrors the state of that. If it is drawn with no detail at all, it may indicate a loss of autonomy or a dependence on something or someone else. If it is drawn with details, then it shows exceptional confidence. Changes can always be made toward self-reliance and self-realization.

Cabin, garden

Should the cabin be near the garden, or if it has garden elements added around it, you recognize your own self-worth and that you are a constant work of art.

If it so happens you drew a cabin like this in a scene that also includes a mountain, it may be an indication of an upcoming journey. It speaks to a love of travel and adventure; someone who recognizes the magnitude of new experiences and of taking time away for renewal.

Cabin, desert

If you placed a cabin in the desert, it may represent a feeling of protection or security. It may further speak to embracing the benefits of solitude.

Alternatively, if the cabin is ramshackle or abandoned in a dry, lifeless, flat desert, it would indicate the opposite to be true, perhaps with resentment of being on one's own or inability to overcome loneliness. If this happens to be the case, know that awareness alone can be the impetus to change direction if open to it, and allow benefits and healing to come in instead.

Cabin, mountain

If you added a cabin to a mountain scene, it indicates you know yourself well enough to get through life's ups and downs. What you do not know, you try to learn or are resourceful to seek out help.

A HOT AIR BALLOON

Opting to add the hot air balloon represents spiritual development and indicates this is of importance at present. Particulars about the balloon's appearance and position influence the overall meaning.

If the balloon is **in the sky** it is about a growing spirituality. There is ongoing intention or work being done to align to soul self.

A balloon **tethered to the ground** would indicate there is hesitation toward the next step or stage of spiritual growth. It could represent feelings of under-preparedness for what comes next; wanting to get it all spot-on and overthinking it.

In the case of a **deflating** hot air balloon, it represents being in a stage where there is a shift of principles taking place. It may be about changing viewpoints, seeing one's life or lifestyle in a different way. There may be a period of coming to terms with the "old ways."

If the hot air balloon is the **largest subject** in the picture, it would suggest false spirituality, ego, and pride. It may reflect the personality needing everyone else to know how spiritual they are, but in fact are insecure about it, or trying to be what they are not. On the brighter side, it would be a sign of being on the brink of breaking free of ego, realizing humility is a choice. Alignment to higher self is at stake.

Hot air balloon, garden

If you added a hot air balloon to a garden scene, spirituality is not only a major factor in life, but it is your life; there is no going backwards to being oblivious. There is acknowledged distinction between your spiritual whole and your human self. Measuring aspects of life against both versions of self for the sake of personal improvement.

Hot air balloon, desert

Drawing the hot air balloon in a desert scene is about wanting to make a change for yourself. Your heart guides your transformation. An inner need exists to understand how this life is the human experience of a spiritual being.

Hot air balloon, mountain

If you chose the hot air balloon for your mountain scene, it represents relying on your intuitive nature to overcome obstacles. If it is a single mountain peak, it may indicate a specific situation you wish you could soar past and not have to deal with.

A CACTUS

If you decided on the cactus for your drawing, it carries symbolism of the enduring spirit, of immortality. It may hold a message about natural defenses and protection. Its condition and where it appears in your picture reveal ideas about this. Should the cactus be **flowering,** there is an unexpected reward or good news coming soon.

When the cactus is the **largest aspect** of the picture, it represents feeling a need to be defensive, to stand your ground, or to let your voice be heard. It is important this is justified and not unwarranted aversion or hostility, so as to not allow outer influences to alter the truest version of you.

If your cactus is **prickly all over**, it is about being guarded or cautious not to repeat cycles that your soul has already worked its way through and learned about. It is acquired strength and wisdom through life experiences.

Cactus, garden

If you paired the cactus with your garden scene, it is about creating personal boundaries and bringing your best self forward. It is a letting go of what no longer serves your highest good.

A cactus drawn in the center of the garden is about intentional focus on making improvements and allowing for change and betterment. It speaks to your flexibility and adaptability.

Cactus, desert

If you placed the cactus in its obvious natural habitat, it is about practicality. It regards a situation you may believe you are "only being realistic" about. But overall, it is about thriving and persevering over time and through lifetimes. It implies that you can apply those strengths to any conditions you face. These are means to a successful outcome.

Cactus, mountain

A pairing of the cactus to a mountain scene signifies preparedness for facing an upcoming challenge. This may be a necessary change that has been in the making for some time. Or, it indicates decisions necessitated because of someone else's actions.

A cactus added directly on the mountain is about facing a drastic situation with resoluteness. It implies survival despite harsh conditions.

A MAN

For this activity, the man is included as a representation of love in your life; possibly a kindred mate, or a significant other (by any gender or identity). In the tarot portion of this activity that follows, this idea of love or the person will be represented by one of the knights.

If the man is the largest subject in the picture, there could be excess importance placed on external validation; expecting another person to make you feel loved or happy, rather than creating this for oneself. Attend to love of self first, and he will deflate to a normal size.

Man, garden

In the case that the man is in the garden, love comes into your life as one part of abundance. Undoubtedly there is a mutual respect for each other's spiritual growth and that part of your soul agreement is about supporting one another toward achievements in life according to your soul plans. This love is your lobster.

If he is in a garden that is barren or weedy, then it may be a sign of lost love, unrequited love, or regret in love relationships.

However, if he is standing next to, yet outside the garden, there is a disconnect in the relationship somehow, or perhaps your paths have not yet crossed.

Man, mountain

When the man is on the mountain, there is an implication of a dilemma with love.

If he is at the bottom of the mountain, it may represent giving up on love too soon or too easily; or it could be about a slump in a relationship.

When he looks like he is trying to walk around the mountain, there is an element of avoidance. It may signify going about a relationship in a roundabout way.

If the man ended up close to the edge of the paper and the mountain stands between him and the other subjects of the drawing, the person represented is not likely to be known until another situation is completed or resolved; this is someone arriving in the future.

A man that is equal in size/height to the mountain is a message that love conquers all.

Man, desert

If the man is drawn walking in a dry desert, it implies loss in or of a love. This does not necessarily represent a current situation; it may instead be about a past loss that has not been healed. Alternatively, it may indicate an extensive period of trying to find a love or an equal partnership in love.

Man, hot air balloon

If he is in the hot air balloon, love and spirituality go hand-in-hand. This represents an equal, a kindred spirit. Should the man be located directly under the hot air balloon, it may indicate a relationship situation where one person is growing apart from the other as their awakening spirit is growing. Perhaps the person is not understanding or respectful toward the transformation.

Man, cactus

A man in the shade of the cactus may indicate a need for a break from dating, or conversely, that a romantic getaway is long overdue. Another possibility is that it implies desperate times, and is encouraging a leap of faith, toward trying new ways to meet people. Let love into your life however it may arrive (romance, friendships, meaningful interactions, etc.). Set all expectation aside.

Man, cabin

In the event that the man was drawn inside the cabin (assuming it is a pristine cabin), it implies a rare love, a once in a lifetime kind of love. This indicates a connection between two people on a soul-level foundation, based on absolute trust, security, and mutual respect.

If the man is **inside a perfect cabin** *and* **the cabin is inside the beautiful garden**, this is the unicorn of all loves. You have intentionally made room in your life for each other because you *want* to share life together, not because you *need* each other to survive. You are completely whole people independently. Do not take it for granted.

However, if he is **closest to the cabin**, but still outside of it, this represents your caution to allow love into your life and discernment toward who you allow in as well.

A BUNNY

The bunny is intended to represent success, especially as manifested through a carefree, faithful spirit.

If the bunny is **hopping**, success comes in increments. Hopping toward or sitting alongside the man (or the man holding the bunny) implies children/family as part of the relationship.

A bunny **hiding** in the picture denotes abundance and success that may not be obvious or immediate.

When the bunny is drawn **closest to the mountain**, or on the mountain, it represents success by way of hard work and overcoming odds; it may feel like luck is involved, but that is just preparation from the hard work combined with a divinely timed opportunity.

The bunny being **closest to the cabin** implies self-made success, possibly through entrepreneurship or straightforward determination.

If the bunny is drawn **in or on the hot air balloon**, or unpredictably in the sky, what were you thinking? A flying bunny? Monty Python fan? In jest of course, because it is fitting. Bunnies are all about creativity and the unexpectedness of one mid-air is an absolute sign of that. Furthermore, it indicates success and abundance derived from your creative spirit, possibly through an artistic venture or a job that entails working with your hands.

A BEE

At last we come to our bee, who is intended to represent how harmony, bliss, and joy come into or are part of your life experience. How does it look and fit into your overall picture? The feeling or thoughts you have about it are worth trusting but use the following references to sort out general meanings.

If the bee is **flying** above the other subjects, it is telling of a natural ebb and flow of joy in life; cleverness at finding joy all around you. In part this is due to knowing that incoming happiness is generated by outgoing gratitude.

In the case of a bee **flying at or buzzing around the man**, it may imply discord in love. But, if it is buzzing **around the cactus**, it is trying to get your attention to say, "Do not fret, things will get better."

If the bee is **on the ground**, there may be a temporary pause in feeling surrounded by harmony, but it is nothing to worry about. Unless you drew the bee about to be stepped on by the man. Then it is demonstrative of a major setback in a love relationship. Hey, it is okay to be upset.

No one wants that bee to get squished. There is still time to upright the relationship issue.

A bee **on/in the garden** is about spiritual harmony, and a deep inner peace is yours to hold on to for keeps. If it is sitting on a flower is a sign of true optimism and a fulfilled spirit.

If the bee is **closest to the mountain**, it is meant to let you know that diligence toward a time-consuming undertaking is going to be joyful or result in joy.

If the bee is **closest to the hot air balloon**, the effort you make toward understanding your spiritual nature and focusing on your life purpose will be positively delightful.

☉ ☉ 🦋 ☉ ☉

After you have collected all the information that applies to your drawing, move on to the tarot portion of the activity which follows. Know that it still works if you want to take a break before continuing.

NO PEEKING SECTION

TELL ME MORE TAROT

Before you shuffle, take the four Knights out of your tarot deck, and set them aside. Use the spread explained below. You may shuffle, cut the deck, and draw the cards however you wish.

There are no additional hidden meanings but take into account those initial symbols you spot. If a card makes sense to you when you first see it, rely on that inner knowingness, *claircognizance*, over a scripted guidebook meaning or even what is included here about the Knights.

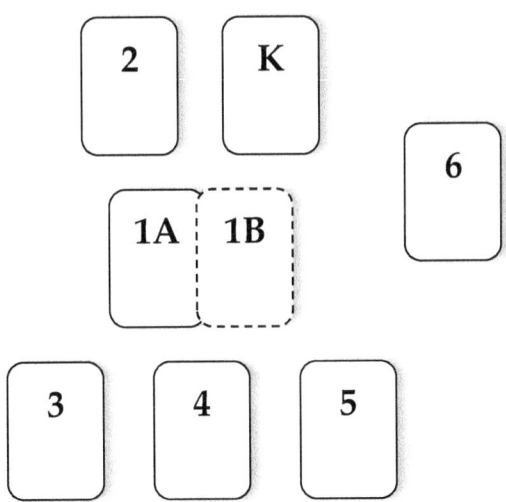

Card(s) 1A, (1B): Tell me more about the scene. Draw only one card per subject included your picture:
   Mountain: for knowledge and challenges,
   Garden: for abundance and spirituality,
   Desert: for personal autonomy and independence.

Card 2 + Knight: Tell me more about my love; which knight is this? Draw one card. For the purpose of this tarot reading, the suit of Card 2 pairs with the Knight of that suit. Move the corres-ponding knight card into the "K" space. This signifies the active energy the person brings to the relationship.

> **Knight of Wands:** creative energy, sense of humor, spontaneity, a positive outlook.
> **Knight of Cups:** romance, affection, generosity, imagination, and devotion.
> **Knight of Swords:** adventure, intellect, safety, challenging you to go beyond the comfort zone.
> **Knight of Pentacles:** constancy, dependability, security, patience, thoughtfulness.

The knight is used intentionally to represent the person's active influence in the relationship, regardless of identity or gender. Include information about the person or the relationship related to the card if you wish or leave it at the above notation.

If you drew a major arcana card for Card 2, and not a suit, still interpret the meaning of the card, but leave the "K" space empty. Added knowledge about this person is not meant to be disclosed yet through one of the Knight pairings. Perhaps it would somehow be misleading. Take what you can from Card 2 on its own for now.

Cards 3, 4, 5: Tell me about my spiritual growth, joy, and how creativity plays a part in my life (one card each).

Card 6: A Summary Message

AFFIRMATION

When you finish with your tarot spread and record your interpretations in your journal, a nice way to wrap up the exercise is to close with an affirmation. Base it on what was covered in or learned about through the Sketchy Too activity. An uncomplicated affirmation, such as, "I experience (love, joy, harmony, spiritual awareness, success, or abundance) and am grateful for every bit of it," is ideal. Decide on one that is meaningful solely for you.

READING FOR YOURSELF

As people tend to discover, it is different using cards for yourself than reading them for someone else. There is a simple explanation for this. When you draw cards for another person you must articulate your ultra-sensory experience, thoughts, feelings, and imagery. If it were only about the cards, you both plainly see them; that would be enough. Intuited, properly used tarot, is largely about what is not visible and the distinctive aspects in the moment, which is what you give the other person a thorough description of. When you do a spread for yourself, that explanation part does not happen. By your own claircognizance, you know what a card means when you flip it over. It may feel uneventful or quick. It should. You are cutting out the bulk of the practice. This is where journaling afterward is effective and gratifying. It necessitates granting yourself similar, introspective attention to detail. The importance lands on the contemplation. That is as it should be, using it as a tool to expand self-awareness.

SNAPSHOT Symbolism

Here you have your four photos and the four suit cards drawn from your tarot deck. You have already labeled your pictures, but now add a second caption to that. Your first frame, Picture 1, is the season you are currently in at the time you do the activity; winter, spring, summer, or fall. Pictures 2, 3, and 4 are the other seasons in sequence.

Next, match your tarot cards to your photos based on the seasons they are representative of traditionally. Pentacles are winter. Wands are spring. Cups are summer. Swords are fall. Place your cards accordingly.

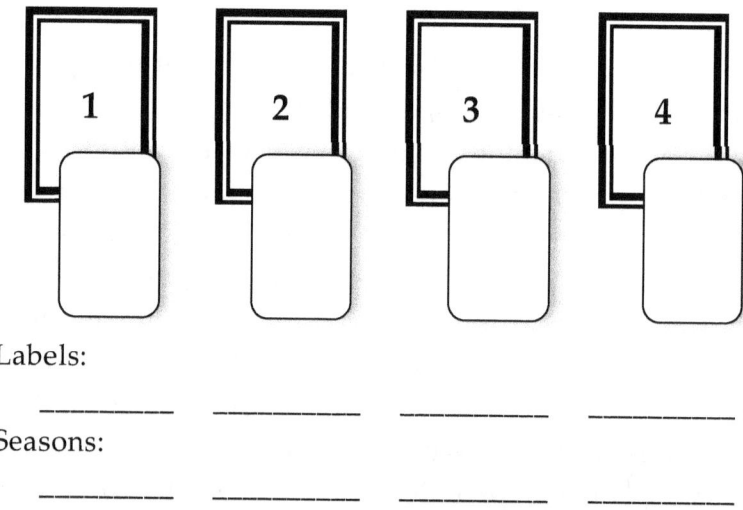

Labels:

———————   ———————   ———————   ———————

Seasons:

———————   ———————   ———————   ———————

The cards paired with the picture symbolism together carry messages related to the snapshot in time you were asking about. It does not reflect on the seasons, as those were just used to make the matches. An exception to this being if your inner voice calls your attention to a situation where a season is a factor, perhaps regarding timing.

NO PEEKING SECTION

Tarot card + your picture symbolism is about:
Pentacles: abundance, income, finances, security, property
Wands: work, projects, endeavors, motivation, energy
Cups: relationships, love, family, emotions, creativity
Swords: intellectual pursuits, communication, decisions

Take a few minutes to journal your interpretations and thoughts about each pairing. Include the symbolic importance of the object you photographed. How does that connect to the meaning behind the card it is matched to?

Keep in mind that if you have asked about a future snapshot, those circumstances and events that have not yet occurred will be impossible to validate until the time has passed. It is fine to not understand what a situation is about or who a person is should a court card appear. There are so many instances, whether using tarot or with direct awareness, where a seed is planted, and the cohesion comes later. Notes should cover the general ideas for now, follow up once the time frame is expended to add to that.

As a partial example, say the first photograph was of a drink coaster on a table. Being winter at the time of the reading, the four of pentacles card pairs with this. Having asked about the distant future, the interpretation suggests that to create future abundance and have security in years to come, it will be important to be frugal, and to make a savings and investment plan. The coaster represents that following the plan will provide a barrier and protection for life's financial events, so there would be less worry or emotional despair (in other words, no water dripping on the table). In this scenario, the second picture would be paired with the wands card for spring, and so on.

TAROT SPY: Part Two

Use the chart below to find out what the cards you selected are meant to represent.

	THE CARD is ABOUT...
A circle	A cycle of personal experience (to be aware of, to focus on, or to break)
Something that looks shiny	An outstanding quality of yours; A strength to enhance or to apply
Is or looks like a vine, cord, ribbon, string, or rope	Your connection to other people
Shows wind, or action/motion/ movement	Your passion(s); what is in your heart; purpose
Something edible	Nurturing your passions, goals, and dreams
Something green	Advice for manifesting or growing passions, goals, and dreams

Write about each card regarding the meaning. Personal symbolism here is substantial. Trust your own thoughts about the interpretations. Use your deck's guidebook to look up generalized meanings if you must.

If a card seems adverse, it may be trying to show a blockage that needs to be cleared to make way for the authentic or positive version. Keep in mind that a reversed card carries its own meaning. It does not automatically mean the opposite of the upright or the negative of the upright. Not all upright cards are propitious of rainbows and kittens either. However, it is up to the interpreter to dig into the layers of meaning to find the purpose and reasoning from a positive viewpoint, because whatever comes up, it is always meant to be helpful, not to impose misfortune or cause a setback. Besides, a negative approach defeats the purpose of encouragement and validation.

This mention is for anyone who has it in mind to only read upright cards. Fear and superstition do not bode well for divination, let alone spirituality. A long-time student was dreadfully averse to cards that appeared upside down and she was missing the entire point. A poor mindset only leads to inaccuracies across the spread. Be practical, use your senses, and do not jump to worst case conclusions.

Think of reversals as doubling the potential meanings, so it is like having 156 cards in a deck rather than 78. Not to mention that when you look at an inverted picture it carries different symbolism. Objects appear interestingly, possibly even distorted to look like things they may or may not have been intended to, offering new points of view and more options to decipher. It certainly becomes intriguing, all the added potential. If a regular deck is not enough challenge, find the *Vice Versa Tarot*, by Lunaea Weatherstone and Massimiliano Filadoro or *Tarot of the Secret Forest* by Lucia Mattioli. With double-sided cards, these decks are at the next level, with upright and reversals amounting to 312 variations.

In the event you are stuck on a meaning for your Tarot Spy cards, ask the Universe for comprehension to come and do not worry. Divine timing has a way of overseeing everything.

TAROT SPY MISSION: Top Secret

FUTURE YOU

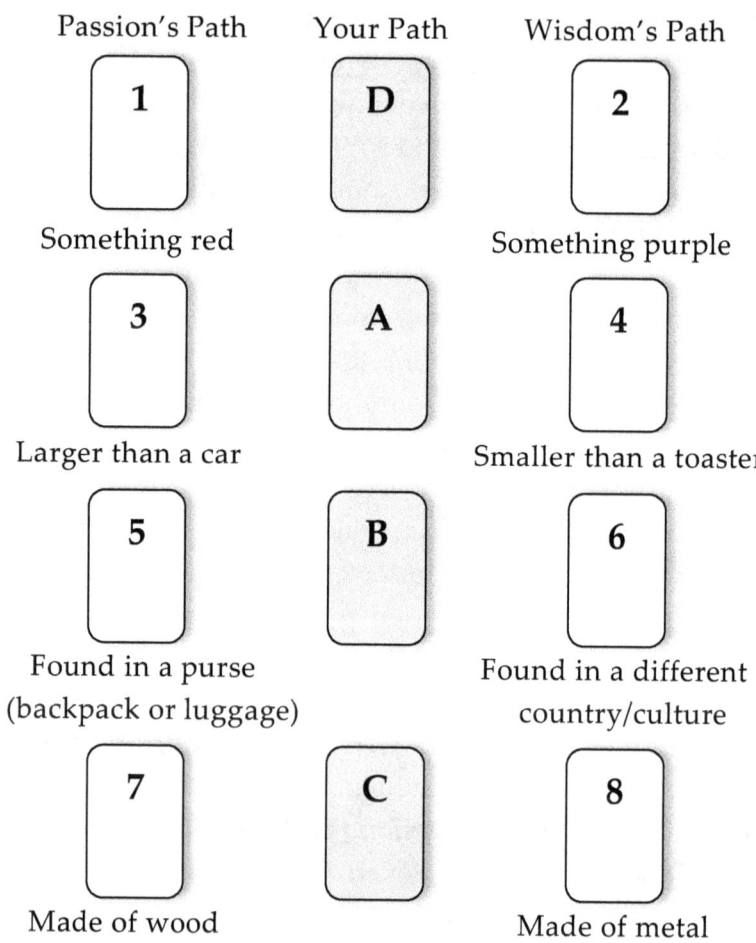

* Please note: The top center card, D, is saved for last. *

Find the cards from each row that you placed in the center column, along with their values following. Base your analyses on those findings.

NO PEEKING SECTION

A

If **Card 3**: This is in reference to an event that your heart is overjoyed by in the future. It is what you are thrilled to have the fortune to experience.

If **Card 4**: This is about seeing fine, magical details in an experience yet to come. It is about synchronicity and spirit, seeing the interconnection of all things.

B

If **Card 5**: This is what you keep close in the future. It is probable that it is a person, situation, or aspiration with a thread of importance running throughout your life.

If **Card 6**: This is about what is beyond to learn from, grow, and explore. A new experience or opportunity yet to come to fruition.

C

If **Card 7**: This is what keeps you grounded, authentic, and self-aware in the future.

If **Card 8**: This is what gives you strength, reinforces your goals, or is a foundation for continued development.

D

If **Card 1**: This is what grows wisdom in your life where there is already love.

If **Card 2**: This is what grows love in your life where there is already wisdom.

Lastly, determine if more cards came from Passion's Path (the left-side column) or Wisdom's Path (the right-side column).

If **equal** (two and two), this is auspicious for a balanced future, both wise and inspired.

If **more from Passion's Path**, your future is likely guided by your heart, and it is worth balancing leaps of faith and carefree spirit with calm, thoughtfulness, observation, and time for solitude.

If **more from Wisdom's Path**, your future is apt to be guided by your purpose and is beneficial to balance the pursuit of endeavors and a dutiful spirit, with humor, time to play, and moments of celebration and gratitude.

Keep a record of your reading, results, and assessments in your journal.

NO PEEKING SECTION

TAROT SPY SOLITAIRE Part Two

Now you have your cards sorted into five separate columns, excluding those in the discard pile.

Pick up all the cards from the first column, shuffle them and place them back as a stack, face down. Repeat that with all the columns of cards until you have five piles.

Reveal the top card of each stack, placing it on top. When you turn over cards, and this goes for all tarot practice at any time, always do this in the same manner. If you flip top to bottom, bottom to top, or side to side, it does not matter. Everyone makes their own natural gesture. It is only important that you always do it one way. The reason is that it affects card reversals, so if you consistently flip the same, there is no mix-up.

When you have all five cards facing up, see the values of the cards below that were predetermined for doing a reading. Add journal notes of your interpretations.

REPRESENTATIONS

Card 1: An opportunity coming.
Card 2: What new ideas/aspects this may bring to your life.
Card 3: Your role with the opportunity.
Card 4: What you ought to know in advance of the opportunity arriving.
Card 5: Information or a clue about another person associated with the opportunity.

TAROT ZOO Continued

Gather news about the zoo you assembled and find out how the cards are important, proceeding here with two additional steps. Begin with finding out about those cards you have placed facing upwards in front of you. At this time only one of the sets should be visible to you, with the remaining six, representing the other enclosures, stacked face down still.

PART TWO: Interpreting the Cards

From the diagrams shown on page 182, find the highlighted enclosure that matches the one you chose. Every sector is assigned to a day of the week, along with a theme or topic.

The cards in the pile corresponding to the enclosure are intended to carry insights on the topic with up to a one-month time frame. For this step, review the cards overall, not as much the animals. We do come back to the animals in the final part.

Looking at your cards that you put in a row facing up, journal some notes about them individually. The values are below.

1. The **first card** in the row is about **what to be aware of** regarding (the designated theme).
2. The **second card** in the row is about **taking action or being observational.**

NO PEEKING SECTION

3. The **third card** in the row is about **what is in your true interest.**
4. The **fourth card** in the row is for **added advice.**

Values that do not have a card to pair with it should be disregarded.

Say you chose the top right enclosure, which happened to have two cards in it. You would read this as:

For one month, regarding *Health, Exercise, Diet, Emotional & Physical Well-Being,* Card 1 shows what I should be aware of and Card 2 is about how to either take action or be observational. Since there are no third and fourth cards, that is all for this part.

If for some reason you chose an enclosure that you had not placed any cards in, your message for now is simply, "All is well." Try the activity for insight again another day when you are drawn to do so.

Once you have finished your interpretation for Part Two, put the face up cards you were using back in their "enclosure" space, face down. You can then proceed to the Part Three instructions that are found after the diagrams.

50 AWARENESS ACTIVITIES & TAROT GAMES — H. Oelschlager

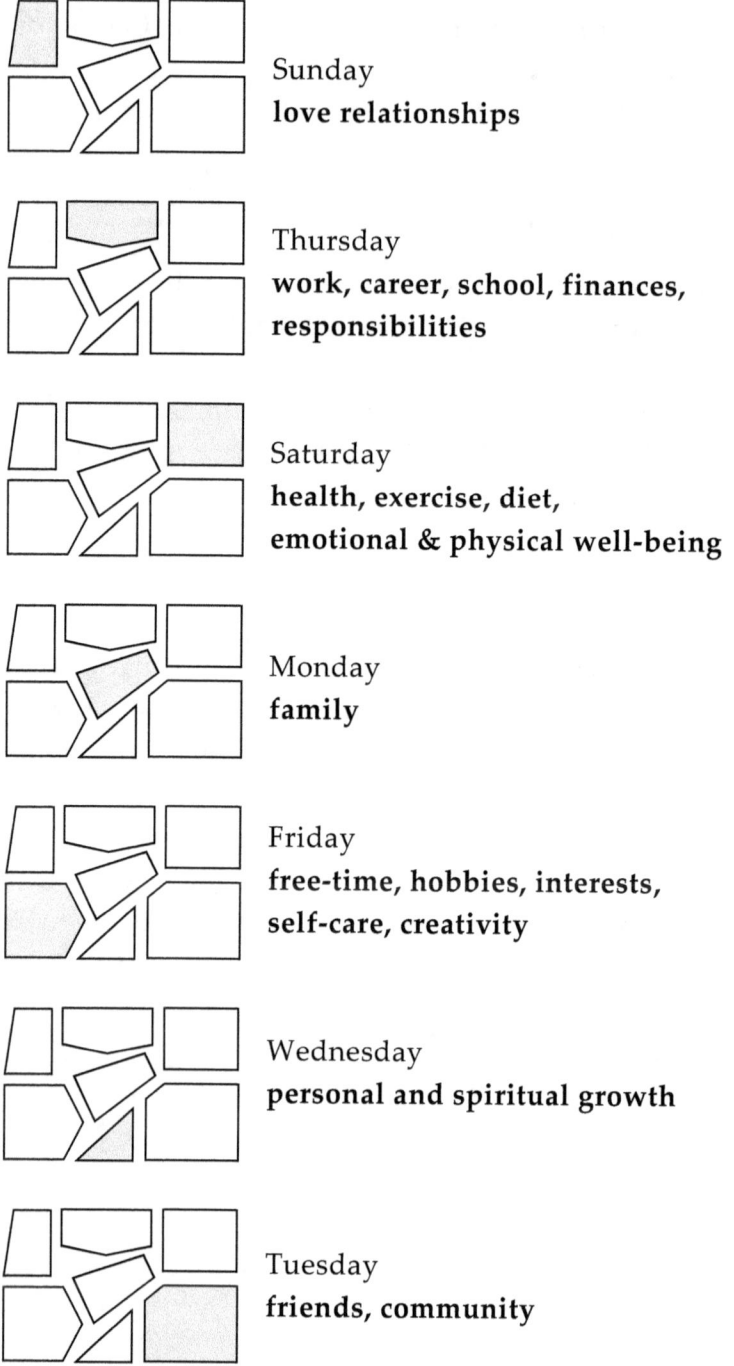

Sunday
love relationships

Thursday
work, career, school, finances, responsibilities

Saturday
health, exercise, diet, emotional & physical well-being

Monday
family

Friday
free-time, hobbies, interests, self-care, creativity

Wednesday
personal and spiritual growth

Tuesday
friends, community

NO PEEKING SECTION

PART THREE: The Animal Signs

Now that your card interpretation is completed, refer to the diagrams. Find the highlighted space matching the day it is *tomorrow* and choose the pile in that position. If this is the "enclosure" you were working with earlier, use the same cards. It is time to study the animals you originally identified in each card.

If no cards happen to be in the enclosure assigned to tomorrow, then consider the zoo closed for the day, but return to visit the Tarot Zoo activity another day.

For the rest, list the animals you identified from the set of cards in your journal (one to four of them). Look up the keywords of animals in the Animal Symbolism Guide (page 197) and note those. The most common animals in card decks are listed, so if one unique to your deck is not included, first, check your guidebook. The author may have given reasons for the symbolism. If still no luck, refer to the resources mentioned in the Appendix.

Now, the animals are meant to apply to the same time frame as the cards you interpreted in Part Two. Their symbolism may give you extra validation, but on top of that, you may see them pop up as signs to keep you going. Animals share the wisdoms they embody. The signs do not need to be actual animals either. Artwork, designs, pictures, videos, and other writing are all around us so they may be represented in those ways. Provided that you are not actively looking for them to appear, they count as signs. A true sign comes with an element of surprise.

THAT'S a LITTLE SKETCHY Evaluation

The second part to the sketching activity is interpreting the symbolism of your picture. It is up to you to evaluate by looking up each of the applicable sections on the following pages. General symbolism tied to the subject's appearance in the overall picture is the basis.

If there is an exceptional aspect to your picture, interpret what you think it means based on the basic meanings provided paired with your own thoughts related to personal symbolism. Make notes and write a summary statement based on the interpretations. Ask your higher self to bring clarity in the following days if it is warranted.

A TREE

Overall, the tree represents growth.

If you drew a **deciduous** tree, one that loses its foliage seasonally, it is about strength, wisdom, and prosperity; providing it is a healthy-looking tree with leaves, that is. It is indicative of a phase of well-being and constancy.

A tree drawn **without leaves**, only the trunk and branches, instead represents a lack of results as far as prosperity or a feeling of delay or stagnancy in life, revolving around your question. Perhaps progress is at a standstill or there is a feeling of being off-track. It may represent a slowing down, such as being between jobs or relationships.

If you drew a **coniferous** tree (evergreen), this is about life and abundance. It may represent a consistent, stable, reliable, secure, or unchanging situation.

POSITIONS

In the event the **tent is between the tree and the pond,** there is work to be done before the reward comes in. This may be a vacation, a raise, or another need-filling benefit.

For the **pond being between the tent and the tree,** the message is that taking a break or vacation may be beneficial to maintain or revitalize the growth energy.

When the **tree is between the pond and the tent,** especially if the tree is proportionately bigger than the pond and/or tent, it may indicate there is excessive focus placed on work. It would be prudent to create balance in life between work, personal, and family life (time for pleasure in general). But with a proportionate tree, it may be a simple reminder to maintain balance.

A TENT

This represents a temporary circumstance or what is in transition. In that regard, it may be about what comes next. Also, make an observation about the condition of the tent in your notes; this parallels the ease or difficulty of change.

If the tent is **staked down** it signifies that what is temporary or transitional is secure or for the purpose of added security.

A tent that is drawn **tethered to the tree** indicates that which is temporary or transitional is a necessary part of growth. There is support through a period of adjustment.

Whether the **door** is open or closed may indicate that what comes next is now available and progressing, versus what has not been revealed yet.

The **proportion** of the tent compared to other parts of the picture may correlate to a transition having a big or little impact, or of how long it lasts.

A CAMPFIRE

The campfire represents partnership, companionship, sharing, and connection with at least one other person, in relationship to your question.

If the fire is **burning**, it may indicate nighttime and that some segments of the whole are hidden or unknown. Although, what is meant to be is already in action and trusting that is important.

An **unlit** firepit, showing only stones and/or logs, may indicate it is daytime, symbolizing that you know all you ought to know about the situation at this time.

If the campfire is **closest to the tree**, it may represent a working relationship or common goals that are or come to result in creating abundance and prosperity. It could indicate a long-term connection and partnership.

A campfire situated **closest to the tent** may represent a connection with a person that is meant to serve a specific purpose, such as working together on a joint project, or a relationship intended for support, healing, and growth in order to move forward.

If the campfire is **closest to the pond**, it symbolizes a mutual appreciation and a connection with a kindred spirit. This would be a common bond that is grounding, stabilizing, or healing.

A POND

The pond symbolizes solitude, emotional healing and balancing. A vacation or respite. Attending to personal well-being. Time for reflection.

The **size** of the pond may indicate how significant your need for personal downtime is. If it is the largest aspect of the picture, you are overdue for a break. If it is the smallest of the five subjects in the picture, including the bird, then you may have forgotten how to put yourself first.

If the pond is **colored-in darkly**, something is being suppressed emotionally that needs tending to for healing and balance.

When there are **waves** in the pond, take note of what is in flux or causing concern that is out of your control.

If the pond goes **around the tree**, with the tree in the middle like an island, you and your future are safe and protected. But, beware of overprotectiveness or defensiveness that may keep others at a distance from you.

If the pond looks **calm and peaceful**, all is well.

A BIRD

Your goals and aspirations are represented by the bird. If you drew a distinct species of bird, check the Animal Symbolism Guide, page 197, for added keywords.

If the bird is **in the tree**, this denotes a present growth phase. Plans are in progress. If you elaborated and put the bird into a nest in the tree, it is about being on a dedicated track with your passions and purpose.

A bird **in the pond** alludes to expect great happiness.

For a bird that is **on the ground**, it implies some views that are still being evaluated. This may be a planning or groundwork phase. There may be some decisions to be made and it is a time to be grounded and thoughtful. Related to your question, a precise goal or dream may not have taken off yet.

Should the bird appear **closest to the campfire**, it may have to do with suppressing your will for someone else's sake. Use caution that you do not depend on another for your happiness. Be conscious of not giving up your goals and dreams for someone else to only have theirs. Also, be mindful of not living out someone else's expectation for you in place of following your true passion and purpose. Compromise is different than surrender.

When the bird is **on the tent**, it is a message that being observational through this time is beneficial.

If the bird is **flying**, you are manifesting your dreams.

NO PEEKING SECTION

THROUGH a TELESCOPE Card Values

Beginning with card number two, compare the assigned values to your notes, adding insights as you go. Work your way clockwise through to the ninth card. When you are finished, the final note is about your center card (#1).

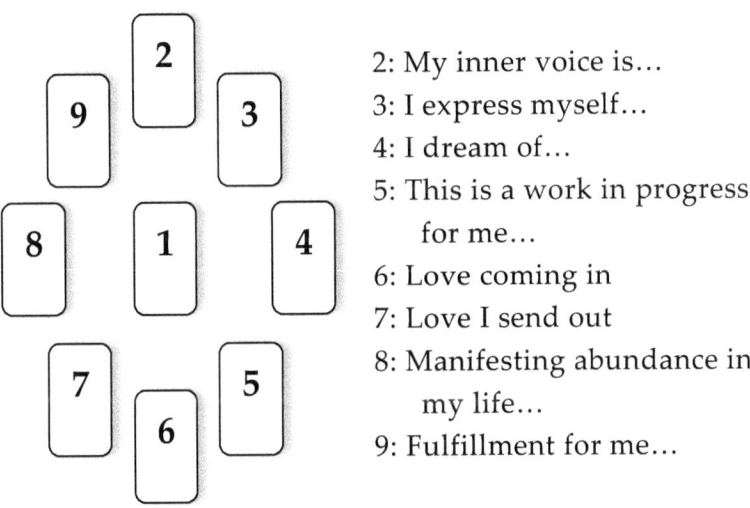

2: My inner voice is…
3: I express myself…
4: I dream of…
5: This is a work in progress for me…
6: Love coming in
7: Love I send out
8: Manifesting abundance in my life…
9: Fulfillment for me…

1: This card is to be read strictly for the positive. This is about the good in you that you may not allow yourself to accept fully. It is you through a telescope. When people say, "I wish you could see yourself through my eyes," they identify you like this. If it gives a negative impression, it is emphasizing that you do not allow your-self to see. Turn the card how it feels positive to you and leave it that way to close your session. Let yourself see. You are an original, Divine creation. You are important and you are loved.

TIMES are a-CHANGIN' Interpretation

Intended values for the card positions are shown below. Pair these to the descriptions you wrote and use them to interpret a clearer meaning behind each card you drew. If the essence of it seems off or negative, try to think of what it may be trying to show you from a different perspective. For example, it may be pointing out that there is a delay, resistance, or blockage, but that all the ingredients are there for the opposite good to manifest itself. A change of understanding, attitude, approach, or action may generate a shift in course for the best outcome.

As always, if there is uncertainty, ask for guidance to come. Using meditation to expand on the information is an option, as well.

Card 1: Who I was before.
This is about strengths, skills, interests, or disposition.

Card 2: Things left behind or forgotten that I may consider bringing back into my life if they serve a renewed purpose.

Card 3: Things I miss dearly or that I struggle to leave behind, even if the separation enables moving forward. There is gratitude to be found here.

Card 4: What I no longer need or want.

Card 5: In leaving aspects behind, it makes room for this instead.

NO PEEKING SECTION

Card 6: What this transformation creates and how it is intended to improve my life.

Card 7: Who I am becoming
This is about your growth and the application of your strengths and passions to your life and connection with others.

Et voilà. You have done a tarot reading for yourself. Yeah, sure, you might have looked at your guidebook. Maybe you did not approach it as we would in a class, relying wholly on your ultra-sensory ability and your connection to higher self, spirit guides, and universal wisdom. But for today, however you went about it, it totally counts. Well done.

WHEEL of COLORFUL FORTUNE Values

Find the colors of your final set below. Use the associations listed as the foundation to interpret each card. Trust your inner voice. Keep it simple. And as always, try your best to come to your own conclusions before resorting to generic guidebook meanings. At the end, look to the bottom of the list for a potential bonus.

Red: a matter of some urgency that needs your attention. Solve the puzzle.

White: something to bring you peace; healing. (If a negative, it shows that resolving what it symbolizes has restorative worth.)

Blue: something to share or something to communicate. Spell it out if you must.

Brown: the support or foundation; what to take with you moving forward.

Orange: related to your creative energy, inspired thinking, manifesting. Go big.

Black: something to meditate or reflect on; time for contemplation. Finding clarity through solitude.

Yellow: related to finding your bliss and joy; a key happiness for your life (may show a theme, like family or travel; something important you should not sacrifice).

Green: a focus; a developing aspect. New growth after a loss or challenge. Indicates what is transforming. Good stuff is brewing.

Pink: something to be open to; a new perspective, way, idea, or prospect. May reveal something or someone to embrace. Ooh la la.

Gray: cannot be bothered with this currently. Something to put off for the moment. A resource-depleting aspect (of time, energy, health, finances, etc.).

BONUS

Did you notice that purple was not included in the color wheel? That is because it may be your bonus card. If you can spell out P-U-R-P-L-E using only the letters in the title of your five cards, then you may draw a sixth card. It does not need to have purple in the design. To be clear, there must be two P's in the letters, you cannot count one twice.

Purple: rewards and blessings are coming; results of hard work, gratitude, and intention manifesting. Let the Universe show you the miracles!

WORD-FILL to FIND INSIGHT Solution

First, double check that you numbered every word in the list as you filled in the puzzle. Then, compare your completed puzzle against the solution that follows. Cross out to exclude any words that landed in wrong spots. They are not to be thought of as mistakes or errors, only that this time they are not to be incorporated into the end results.

NO PEEKING SECTION

For the next part, fill in the blanks using the words that correspond to the order you completed them in the initial puzzle. Leave spaces blank for misplaced words.

#27 _____ This represents a key theme for this week or month.

#1 _____ This set of three represents current priorities.
#4 _____
#7 _____

#18 _____ What you may wish to leave for later or should not worry about.
#21 _____
#24 _____

#11 _____ What brings you into alignment with your higher self currently.

#14 _____ Where transformation may be occurring.

#17 _____ What might bring balance if you increase this aspect.

To grow that last aspect (#17), you may want to write an affirmation using that word (or a derivation) as a tool. Only do so if it personally feels correct and positive. In which case, use one of the following examples or create your own.

"I am _____."
"I have _____."
"My life is filled with _____."

Think of your affirmation over the coming days until you feel that you have achieved this balance.

This activity may be repeated, of course, when enough time has passed that you are able to complete the word-fill without preconception to placing the words. Start with a freshly printed puzzle and you will be ready to go.

ANIMAL SYMBOLISM GUIDE

This list includes symbolism keywords relevant to certain animals and animal spirits. As you read the listed words pertaining to an animal, see which one stands out to you in the moment. Not all of them apply in a single given circumstance.

Animals and their wisdoms have been unavoidably skimmed down for the guide. Neither to disparage the rest of the 1.6 million identified species or the 65,000 vertebrates alone, nor to exasperate any human. If you do not find an animal you are searching for or if you would like further information about animal spirits, give the resources listed in the Appendix a try.

After that, if you still cannot find a representation, it most certainly calls for meditation to investigate such an exceptional predicament. Or, bypass it all straightaway to meditate, listen to your higher self, and learn about the animal wisdom in a private context.

All animals, including those that are extinct or mythological, potentially bring personal and spiritual meaning to us through their symbolism. When they appear in our lives, they carry messages to us to let us know what they are trying to help us notice, learn, exemplify, or exude.

ANIMAL SYMBOLISM GUIDE

◎ A-B-C ◎

Ant: diligence, patience, planning, routine, burden

Bear: instinct, introspection, leadership, motherhood

Bee: concentration, interconnection, prosperity, rebirth

Birds (general): a new perspective, freedom, flexibility, joy, harmony, balance, love

Bison, Buffalo: abundance, courage, generosity, survival, challenge, provision

Blue Jay: messages of guidance, spiritual growth, using caution, planning diversion

Butterfly: hopefulness, joy, creativity, reincarnation, transformation, romance, spirituality, awakening

Cat: clairvoyance, a healing nature, independence, love

Chimpanzee: intelligence, problem-solving, compassion

Coyote: Stealth, deception, removing masks to become authentic, humor toward own mistakes

Crab: finding uses for secondhand items, protection over home, being able to change direction

Crayfish, Lobster: strength, perseverance, tenacity, concentration, simplicity, overcoming the mind/ego

Crow/Raven: call to attention, ethics, direction, fearlessness, introspection, new opportunity

◎ D-E ◎

Deer: grace, gratitude and giving, innocence, softness

Dog: companionship, bonds, love, loyalty, vigilance

Dolphin: balance, harmony, optimism, spiritual guidance

Donkey: silliness, stubbornness, decision-making

Dove: peace, harmony, conciliation, love, respect, grace

Dragon: advocating, bravery, destiny, passion, defense

Dragonfly: awareness, dream messages, new viewpoint

Duck: emotional clarity, fertility, stability, stillness

ANIMAL SYMBOLISM GUIDE

Eagle: aspirations, life purpose, positive transition, wisdom, healing, creative spirit, spirituality
Elephant: clairsentience, devotion, family bonds, strength, clearing obstacles

☉ F-G-H-I ☉

Fish: fertility, harmony, regeneration, love, variety
    Catfish (specifically): clairgustance
Fox: ingenuity, innocence, observation, originality
Frog: cleansing, sensitivity, steps to a goal, longevity
Giraffe: communication, premonition, higher awareness
Grasshopper: following passion, health, leap of faith
Gryphon: guardian, insight, leaps of faith, soul-searching
Hawk: creativity, destiny, spirit messages, truth, vigilance, originality, seeing the bigger picture
Heron: diversity, multi-tasking, exploring, self-reliance
Horse: adventure and travel, endurance, passion, sociability, faithfulness, friendship, cooperation
Insects (general): minor obstacles to be overcome

☉ K-L-M-O-P ☉

Kangaroo: adaptability, nurturing, leaps of faith, instinct
Koala: advising, methodical, patience, uncontroversial
Lion: energy, pride, self-fulfillment, superiority, courage, aggression, overcoming stress
Lizard: facing fears, overcoming ego, recovery
Monkey: charm, family bonds, playfulness, unity
Mouse: quietness, being unseen, understanding details
Opossum: neutrality, recognizing gifts, viewpoint
Owl: attentiveness, claircognizance, renewal, self-esteem, wisdom, awareness of hidden things
Panther: beauty, clairaudience, grace, self-empowerment

Pegasus: astral travel, guidance, humility, inspiration
Penguin: patience, endurance, masculine-feminine balance
Phoenix: dignity, perseverance, progress, rediscovery,
    transformation, renewal

☯ R-S ☯

Rabbit: agility, creativity, improving ultra-senses,
    fertility, playfulness, observation
Raccoon: curiosity, dexterity, disguise, seeking guidance,
    self-assurance
Salamander: cooperation, perseverance, secrecy, work,
    endeavors, subtlety, primal energy, creativity, growth
Sheep: kindness, sensitivity, new beginnings, community,
    productivity
Snake: clairolience, instinct, transition, self-reliance,
    vanity, self-righteousness
Spider: agility, creativity, intricacy, knowledge, inspiration
Squirrel: discovery, imagination, prudence, puzzle-solving,
    cleverness, preparation
Swan: grace, devotion, nurturing, accepting change,
    personal/spiritual development, emotional balance

☯ T-U-W ☯

Tiger: bravery, energy, power, leadership, truthfulness
Turtle: clairaudience, clairolience, clairvoyance, patience,
    life, persistence, resilience
Unicorn: artistic ability, dreams/dreaming, inner child,
    peace, mystery, blessings
Whale: assurance, creation, intuition, music for healing
Wolf: intellect, poise, regard for family/community,
    beauty, survival, solitude, self-confidence

APPENDIX

HELPFUL RESOURCES

For guidance in learning meditation and for additional meditations, along with a detailed appendix for interpreting various symbolism, try my first book, *Through the Blue Door: A Medium's Guide to Ultra-Sensory Meditation & Journaling*. Also, look into these options online and in print:

WEBSITES:
Symbols.com www.symbols.com

Animal Energies Dictionary www.wildspeak.com

BOOKS:
Animal Speak: The Spiritual and Magical Powers of Creatures Great & Small. Ted Andrews. Llewellyn, 2002.

Dream Dictionary: An A to Z Guide to Understanding Your Unconscious Mind. Tony Crisp. Dell, 2002.

Pocket Guide to Spirit Animals: Understanding Messages from Your Animal Spirit Guides. Steven Farmer. Hay House, 2012.

Tarot: Plain and Simple. Anthony Louis. Llewellyn, 2002.

Totem Animal Messages: Channeled Messages from the Animal Kingdom. Brigit Goldworthy. Balboa Press, 2013.

The Ultimate Guide to Tarot. Liz Dean. Fair Winds Press, 2015.

What's in Your Dreams: An A to Z Dream Dictionary. Michael Vigo. Lulu.com, 2010.

AN AFTERWORD

May 21.

In April, when I had asked myself the question, "Is it possible to write this entire book in a month, during quarantine of a global pandemic?" The answer is an astonishing, "Yes." Chalk one up for the divine miracles today.

Through the unequivocal gravity in this world, we now witness all that does not serve the evolution of human beings in upheaval so healing may take place. As part of that, some who have been defiant against their true selves are being brought to face their spirituality and soul purpose on this planet. Which leaves it up to those already cognizant to sustain love, to embrace oneness and all that encompasses, staying the course.

But not everything needs to have a serious bent. Life throws enough of that at us. It is good to find ways to engage our spiritual nature, purely to enjoy it. To invest in ourselves through happiness and levity. To connect with others. To laugh as we learn and explore.

While on the surface this book is for the fun and games, it is rooted in two decades of study and work in the field. Metaphysical concepts, numerology, symbology, energy work, meditation, and divination. Applying these tools of self-awareness is a means to equilibrium and enhancement of life experience.

Continue to use this text as a resource to access what your heart desires. Carry that with you, allowing progress. Grant your soul to show you the way to all of it. Observe the signs and the little miracles all around. Begin by waking up in the morning saying, "Show me the good stuff!" Watch what unfolds. Every time you see it, throw a burst of gratitude out to the Universe, because it keeps growing blessings for you. That is one way the cycle of giving and receiving happens. Maybe it becomes your personal superpower.

◎ ◎ 🦋 ◎ ◎

With appreciation and gratitude
…to my guides and loved ones in spirit.
…to those favorite college professors, Will Weaver, and Drs. Anderson, Gurney, Day, Giovenco, and Rotto for growing my love of reading, writing, and all languages.
…to the clients who have thoughtfully supported my small businesses during these challenging times.
…to my BFF since diapers, and my soul sisters, for being all the things (I hope you found your secret messages).
…to my real sister, a real-life hero, who goes above and beyond for every human and especially family.
…and to my son, a pretty terrific, albeit unexpecting, quarantine-mate, not only because you are an awesome chef and adventure buddy. I am ever so proud of you and your accomplishments. Ég elska þig. Go do everything in the world your heart dreams of and make life an amazing journey. And, steer clear of Colin Robinsons.

AN AFTERWORD

Be sure to visit MandorlaAcademy.com. Share your meditation stories and tarot poetry. Sign up for the e-mail list. Take an interactive, online course to keep growing your awareness. In the shop, find the FREE printables to download that accompany activities in this book.

One last tiny note if you have read this far. I snuck a secret fifty-first activity into the book as a thank-you. On the divider pages, the black and white illustrations double as coloring pages. Fill them in with colored pencil as a nice meditative activity if you are so inclined. Use the time spent on it for relaxing or having a chat with your higher self.

Wishing you the wonderful,
Heather

www.MandorlaAcademy.com
facebook.com/minnesotamedium
instagram.com/mandorlaacademy
instagram.com/heatheroelschlager

ABOUT the AUTHOR

Heather Oelschlager is a professional psychic medium and spiritual consultant who lives in southern Minnesota. For twenty years, she has taught comprehensive courses on spiritual development and metaphysical topics. *Through the Blue Door: A Medium's Guide to Ultra-Sensory Meditation and Journaling* is her first book. She is getting through isolation on dark coffee, baking bread, car picnics, photo hikes, bonfire nights, and artsy pursuits.

If you never did you should.
These things are fun and fun is good!"
-Dr. Seuss

ART PRINTS

Art prints of select illustrations from Heather's books, additional artwork, and photography are available for purchase. Visit MandorlaAcademy.com for information.

NOTES

NOTES

www.ingramcontent.com/pod-product-compliance
Lightning Source LLC
LaVergne TN
LVHW021601070426
835507LV00015B/1893